Audit an Compliance in IAM (SOX, GDPR, HIPAA, NIST, ISO 27001)

James Relington

DEDICATION

To my family, whose support and encouragement have been my greatest motivation. To my colleagues and mentors, who have generously shared their knowledge and experience. And to all those passionate about technology and security, who strive to build a safer digital world.

ACKNOWLEDGEMENTS

I would like to express my gratitude to everyone who contributed to the creation of this book. To my family and friends for their unwavering support, to my colleagues and mentors for their valuable contributions, and to the technology community for continually sharing knowledge and pushing the boundaries of innovation. A special thank you to those who reviewed, provided feedback, and inspired me along this journey. Their encouragement and experience have made this work possible.

Introduction to IAM Audit and Compliance

Identity and Access Management (IAM) is a fundamental aspect of modern cybersecurity, ensuring that the right individuals have appropriate access to systems, applications, and data. As organizations increasingly rely on digital infrastructure, IAM has become central to managing security risks, protecting sensitive information, and complying with regulatory requirements. The need for robust IAM frameworks has never been greater, particularly in industries subject to stringent compliance regulations such as SOX, GDPR, HIPAA, NIST, and ISO 27001. Audit and compliance play a critical role in maintaining trust, minimizing risks, and ensuring accountability within IAM programs.

IAM audits are designed to assess whether identity and access controls align with organizational policies and regulatory frameworks. These audits help identify potential vulnerabilities, misconfigurations, and policy violations that could lead to security breaches. By regularly reviewing user access, authentication mechanisms, and privilege management, organizations can proactively mitigate risks and demonstrate compliance to regulatory bodies. The audit process typically involves reviewing logs, access records, and system configurations to verify that access is granted based on predefined rules and that any deviations are justified and documented.

Compliance requirements vary depending on industry regulations, but they generally share common principles related to data protection, access control, and monitoring. SOX (Sarbanes-Oxley Act) focuses on financial data integrity and requires stringent controls over who can access financial systems. GDPR (General Data Protection Regulation) emphasizes user privacy and mandates strict access restrictions on personal data. HIPAA (Health Insurance Portability and Accountability Act) enforces rules for safeguarding healthcare information and ensuring that only authorized personnel have access to patient records. NIST (National Institute of Standards and Technology) provides a cybersecurity framework that includes IAM best practices, while ISO 27001 establishes an international standard for information security management, covering access control policies, authentication mechanisms, and identity governance.

To ensure compliance with these regulations, organizations must implement structured IAM policies that define how identities are created, managed, and deactivated. Identity lifecycle management is a key aspect of IAM compliance, requiring organizations to enforce strict processes for provisioning and deprovisioning users. When an employee joins a company, access should be granted based on their job role, with clear documentation of permissions. Similarly, when an employee leaves or changes roles, their access must be adjusted or revoked in a timely manner to prevent unauthorized access. Failure to properly manage the identity lifecycle can lead to compliance violations and security risks, such as former employees retaining access to critical systems.

Authentication and authorization mechanisms also play a crucial role in IAM audit and compliance efforts. Organizations must enforce strong authentication policies, such as multi-factor authentication (MFA), to reduce the risk of credential-based attacks. Role-based access control (RBAC) and attribute-based access control (ABAC) are common methods used to ensure that users only have access to the resources necessary for their job functions. Regular access reviews and recertification processes help validate that permissions remain appropriate over time. Auditors often examine whether access reviews are conducted periodically and whether access rights are adjusted based on changes in user roles or responsibilities.

One of the most critical aspects of IAM compliance is monitoring and logging user activities. Regulations such as SOX, GDPR, and HIPAA require organizations to maintain detailed logs of access events, authentication attempts, and administrative actions. These logs serve as evidence that access policies are being enforced correctly and provide a means to investigate security incidents. A well-implemented logging strategy should capture relevant information while ensuring that logs are protected from tampering. Centralized logging and integration with Security Information and Event Management (SIEM) systems allow organizations to analyze access patterns, detect anomalies, and respond to potential threats.

Audit readiness is another key factor in IAM compliance. Organizations must maintain comprehensive documentation of their IAM policies, procedures, and controls to demonstrate compliance during audits. This includes maintaining records of user access requests, approvals, and changes to access rights. Automated IAM solutions can streamline compliance efforts by generating audit reports, tracking policy violations, and providing real-time visibility into access management. By leveraging automation, organizations can reduce manual efforts, improve accuracy, and ensure that compliance obligations are met efficiently.

IAM compliance is not a one-time effort but an ongoing process that requires continuous monitoring and adaptation. Regulatory requirements evolve, and organizations must regularly update their IAM policies to address new risks and changes in compliance frameworks. Employee training and awareness programs also play a crucial role in IAM compliance, ensuring that users understand security policies and follow best practices when accessing systems.

The intersection of IAM, audit, and compliance is a complex but essential area for organizations aiming to protect their data and maintain regulatory adherence. By establishing a strong IAM governance framework, implementing robust authentication and authorization mechanisms, and conducting regular audits, organizations can minimize security risks and demonstrate compliance with industry regulations.

The Importance of Compliance in Identity and Access Management

Compliance in Identity and Access Management (IAM) is a fundamental aspect of modern cybersecurity and risk management. Organizations today operate in an environment where data breaches, insider threats, and regulatory fines are increasing concerns. Compliance ensures that IAM processes are structured, standardized, and aligned with regulatory requirements designed to protect sensitive data, mitigate risks, and maintain operational integrity. Whether dealing with financial regulations like SOX, privacy laws such as GDPR, healthcare mandates like HIPAA, or security frameworks such as NIST and ISO 27001, organizations must prioritize compliance to avoid legal penalties, reputational damage, and security vulnerabilities.

IAM compliance is critical because it establishes clear guidelines for how identities are created, managed, and revoked within an organization. Without proper controls, employees, contractors, and third-party users may gain unauthorized access to sensitive systems and data, leading to security breaches. Compliance frameworks require organizations to enforce strict access policies that align with the principle of least privilege, ensuring that users only have the minimum access necessary to perform their job functions. This reduces the risk of data misuse, insider threats, and privilege escalation attacks.

Regulatory mandates exist to address the growing concerns surrounding data privacy and security. Compliance frameworks such as GDPR emphasize the protection of personal data, requiring organizations to implement access controls that prevent unauthorized disclosure. Similarly, HIPAA mandates strict identity and access management practices to safeguard healthcare records. By enforcing compliance in IAM, organizations can establish accountability, ensuring that access is granted and maintained based on documented policies rather than ad-hoc decisions. This level of control helps organizations demonstrate due diligence in protecting sensitive information.

One of the core aspects of IAM compliance is access governance. Organizations must continuously monitor, audit, and review user access to ensure that permissions are appropriate and compliant with regulatory standards. Periodic access reviews help identify anomalies, such as excessive privileges or orphaned accounts, which can pose significant security risks. Automated identity governance solutions enable organizations to streamline compliance efforts by enforcing policy-based access controls, triggering alerts for unauthorized changes, and generating audit reports that regulators require.

Strong authentication mechanisms are another essential element of IAM compliance. Regulations such as NIST and ISO 27001 emphasize the importance of multi-factor authentication (MFA) to prevent unauthorized access. Weak authentication practices, such as relying solely on passwords, increase the likelihood of credential theft and unauthorized account access. By enforcing MFA and other advanced authentication techniques, organizations can enhance security while meeting compliance requirements. This not only protects against cyber threats but also demonstrates a proactive approach to regulatory adherence.

Another key component of compliance in IAM is auditability. Organizations must maintain comprehensive logs of identity-related activities, including user logins, access requests, approvals, and privilege escalations. Regulatory frameworks like SOX require organizations to provide detailed records of user access to financial systems, ensuring transparency and accountability. By leveraging centralized logging solutions and integrating them with Security Information and Event Management (SIEM) tools, organizations can analyze access patterns, detect anomalies, and generate compliance reports efficiently. This proactive approach to audit readiness helps organizations respond effectively to regulatory inquiries and security incidents.

Compliance is also a driver of business trust and reputation. Customers, partners, and stakeholders expect organizations to have strong security controls in place to protect their data. Demonstrating compliance with industry standards reassures clients that their information is being handled securely. Many organizations require their vendors and partners to adhere to strict IAM compliance requirements before engaging in business relationships. A failure to meet these standards can lead to lost business opportunities, decreased customer trust, and potential legal consequences.

Managing IAM compliance is an ongoing process that requires continuous monitoring, adaptation, and training. Regulatory requirements evolve, and organizations must stay ahead of compliance changes to avoid violations. Employees must also be educated on IAM best practices, as human error remains one of the leading causes of compliance failures. Regular training programs help reinforce security policies, ensuring that users understand the importance of following access control guidelines and protecting sensitive information.

IAM compliance is not just about avoiding penalties; it is about creating a secure and well-governed IT environment. Organizations that integrate compliance into their IAM strategies benefit from improved security posture, reduced risk exposure, and enhanced operational efficiency. By implementing structured identity management policies, enforcing strong authentication, conducting regular audits, and staying informed about evolving regulatory requirements, organizations can successfully navigate the complex landscape of IAM compliance while maintaining trust, security, and business continuity.

Understanding SOX Compliance and Its Impact on IAM

The Sarbanes-Oxley Act (SOX) was enacted in 2002 as a response to financial scandals that exposed widespread fraud and mismanagement in corporate accounting practices. Designed to restore investor confidence, SOX imposes strict regulations on publicly traded companies, requiring them to maintain accurate financial records and implement strong internal controls. Identity and Access Management (IAM) plays a crucial role in achieving SOX compliance by ensuring that only authorized individuals have access to financial systems, data, and processes. Organizations must implement robust IAM policies to prevent unauthorized access, ensure accountability, and maintain the integrity of financial reporting.

One of the primary objectives of SOX compliance is to prevent fraudulent activities by enforcing stringent controls over access to financial data. Section 404 of SOX specifically requires companies to establish and maintain internal controls that provide reasonable assurance over the reliability of financial reporting. These controls must be regularly evaluated through audits to confirm their effectiveness. IAM systems are instrumental in meeting these requirements by providing mechanisms for identity authentication, role-based access control, and access monitoring. Without a properly structured IAM framework, organizations risk non-compliance, which can result in financial penalties, reputational damage, and legal consequences.

Role-based access control (RBAC) is a critical aspect of SOX compliance, ensuring that employees have access only to the resources necessary for their job functions. The principle of least privilege dictates that users should be granted the minimum level of access required to perform their duties. This reduces the risk of unauthorized modifications to financial records or intentional fraud. IAM solutions enable organizations to enforce these policies by assigning roles based on job responsibilities and automatically adjusting access rights as employees change positions within the company. Maintaining clear role definitions and access policies simplifies the audit process and demonstrates compliance with SOX regulations.

User authentication and access controls are key components of IAM strategies for SOX compliance. Strong authentication mechanisms, such as multi-factor authentication (MFA), help protect sensitive financial data from unauthorized access. SOX mandates that companies implement procedures to verify user identities before granting access to critical financial systems. Password policies, biometric authentication, and smart card-based authentication are commonly used methods to strengthen identity verification. Organizations must also ensure that authentication credentials are securely managed, minimizing the risk of credential theft or misuse.

Auditability and logging are essential to meeting SOX requirements. Organizations must maintain detailed logs of all access-related activities, including user logins, changes to financial records, and administrative actions. These logs serve as evidence of compliance, providing auditors with a clear trail of user activity. Security Information and Event Management (SIEM) solutions help centralize and analyze access logs, enabling real-time monitoring for suspicious behavior. Automated logging tools streamline the audit process by generating reports that demonstrate compliance with SOX regulations. The ability to detect unauthorized access attempts and respond to security incidents promptly is a key requirement for passing SOX audits.

Separation of duties (SoD) is another fundamental control enforced by SOX to prevent conflicts of interest and reduce the risk of fraud. In IAM, this means ensuring that no single user has excessive privileges that allow them to perform multiple conflicting actions within financial systems. For example, an employee who processes payments should not have the ability to approve those payments. IAM solutions provide mechanisms to enforce SoD by defining access policies that prevent users from holding conflicting permissions. Regular access reviews help organizations identify and remediate SoD violations, ensuring that compliance with SOX standards is maintained.

Periodic access reviews and recertifications are required to ensure that access permissions remain appropriate over time. SOX compliance mandates that organizations regularly review user access to financial systems and revoke access for employees who no longer require it. IAM solutions automate these reviews, allowing managers to approve or reject access requests based on job responsibilities and compliance requirements. Continuous monitoring of user access helps detect anomalies, such as inactive accounts with privileged access, which could be exploited for fraudulent activities. By implementing automated access review processes, organizations can reduce the burden of manual audits and maintain continuous compliance with SOX regulations.

Third-party access management is another critical aspect of SOX compliance. Many organizations rely on external vendors, consultants, and contractors who require access to financial systems. IAM policies must extend to third-party users, ensuring that their access is properly controlled and monitored. Organizations should implement just-in-time (JIT) access provisioning, granting temporary access to third-party users only when necessary and revoking it once their work is complete. Maintaining detailed records of third-party access and enforcing strict authentication requirements help prevent unauthorized access and protect sensitive financial data.

IAM automation enhances SOX compliance by reducing human errors and improving consistency in access management. Manual processes for provisioning and deprovisioning user accounts introduce risks, such as granting excessive privileges or failing to revoke access for former employees. Automated IAM solutions enforce compliance policies by ensuring that access requests follow approval workflows, access rights are assigned based on predefined policies, and changes are documented for audit purposes. Automation also enables organizations to respond quickly to access-related security incidents, minimizing the risk of non-compliance.

Organizations that fail to meet SOX compliance requirements face significant consequences, including regulatory fines, loss of investor trust, and potential legal action. Non-compliance can also indicate broader security weaknesses, increasing the likelihood of data breaches and financial fraud. By integrating IAM best practices into their compliance strategy, organizations can not only meet SOX requirements but also strengthen their overall security posture. IAM ensures that financial data remains protected, access is properly controlled, and auditability is maintained, ultimately supporting the long-term stability and integrity of the business.

GDPR Requirements for Identity and Access Management

The General Data Protection Regulation (GDPR) is a comprehensive privacy law designed to protect the personal data of individuals within the European Union. Enforced in May 2018, GDPR introduced strict requirements for organizations that collect, process, and store personal data. Identity and Access Management (IAM) plays a crucial role in GDPR compliance by ensuring that access to personal data is strictly controlled, monitored, and documented. Organizations must implement IAM policies that align with GDPR's principles, focusing on data minimization, access restrictions, user accountability, and security measures that protect personal information from unauthorized access.

One of the fundamental principles of GDPR is data minimization, which requires organizations to collect and process only the personal data that is necessary for a specific purpose. IAM helps enforce this principle by implementing role-based access control (RBAC) and attribute-based access control (ABAC) to ensure that users only have access to the data they need to perform their job functions. Granting excessive privileges increases the risk of unauthorized data exposure, which can lead to non-compliance. By restricting access based on roles, attributes, and job responsibilities, organizations can limit unnecessary data exposure and reduce the risk of data misuse.

GDPR also mandates strict access controls to prevent unauthorized individuals from accessing personal data. Organizations must ensure that only authorized users, such as employees, contractors, and service providers, can access sensitive information. IAM solutions help enforce access control policies by requiring strong authentication mechanisms, such as multi-factor authentication (MFA), to verify user identities before granting access. Weak authentication practices, such as using simple passwords, increase the risk of credential theft and unauthorized access. By implementing MFA and enforcing password complexity policies, organizations can strengthen access security and meet GDPR requirements.

Another critical requirement of GDPR is the ability to track and audit access to personal data. Organizations must maintain detailed logs of user activities, including login attempts, data access requests, and privilege modifications. These audit logs serve as evidence that access policies are being enforced and provide insights into potential security threats. IAM solutions integrate with logging and monitoring systems to capture access events in real time, allowing security teams to detect anomalies, investigate suspicious activities, and respond to potential data breaches. Maintaining comprehensive access logs is essential for demonstrating compliance and responding to regulatory inquiries.

Data subject rights, such as the right to access, rectify, and delete personal data, are central to GDPR compliance. IAM systems must support mechanisms that allow organizations to manage these requests efficiently. When a data subject requests access to their personal information, IAM solutions help verify the user's identity and ensure that only authorized personnel handle the request. Similarly, when a data subject exercises their right to be forgotten, IAM ensures that their access is revoked, and their data is securely erased from all systems. Automating these processes through IAM reduces administrative overhead and ensures compliance with GDPR timelines.

Consent management is another area where IAM plays a crucial role. GDPR requires organizations to obtain explicit and informed consent before collecting and processing personal data. IAM solutions help enforce consent policies by ensuring that users cannot access or process certain data without documented consent. By integrating IAM with consent management platforms, organizations can track user consents, enforce data processing restrictions based on consent status, and revoke access when consent is withdrawn. Maintaining accurate consent records is essential for demonstrating compliance during audits and regulatory reviews.

The principle of data protection by design and by default, outlined in

GDPR, requires organizations to embed security measures into their systems and processes. IAM supports this requirement by enforcing default access restrictions, ensuring that new user accounts and applications adhere to predefined security policies. Organizations must configure IAM solutions to apply least privilege access, automatic session timeouts, and continuous access monitoring by default. Implementing these security measures from the outset reduces the likelihood of unauthorized data access and strengthens overall compliance.

Third-party access management is another critical aspect of GDPR compliance. Organizations often share personal data with external vendors, service providers, and business partners. GDPR requires organizations to ensure that third parties implement appropriate security measures to protect this data. IAM solutions help manage third-party access by enforcing just-in-time (JIT) provisioning, granting temporary access only when necessary, and revoking access once the task is completed. Organizations must also conduct regular access reviews and risk assessments to ensure that third-party access remains compliant with GDPR requirements.

Incident response and breach notification are essential components of GDPR. In the event of a data breach, organizations must notify regulatory authorities within 72 hours and inform affected individuals if there is a high risk to their rights and freedoms. IAM solutions help organizations detect and respond to security incidents by providing real-time alerts for suspicious access attempts, privilege escalations, and unauthorized data modifications. By integrating IAM with security incident response platforms, organizations can automate breach detection, initiate rapid containment measures, and generate compliance reports required for regulatory disclosures.

Employee training and awareness programs are vital to ensuring that IAM policies align with GDPR compliance. Users must understand the importance of protecting personal data and following access control guidelines. IAM solutions support training initiatives by enforcing security policies, prompting users to review compliance guidelines during login, and requiring periodic security awareness assessments. Educating employees on GDPR requirements helps reduce human errors, which are a common cause of data breaches and compliance violations.

Organizations that fail to meet GDPR's IAM requirements face significant consequences, including hefty fines, legal actions, and reputational damage. Non-compliance can also lead to loss of customer trust and reduced business opportunities. By implementing robust IAM practices, organizations can protect personal data, enforce strong access controls, and demonstrate compliance with GDPR regulations. IAM serves as the foundation for ensuring that personal data remains secure, access is properly managed, and organizations can confidently navigate the complexities of GDPR compliance.

HIPAA Compliance and IAM Best Practices

The Health Insurance Portability and Accountability Act (HIPAA) was enacted to protect the privacy and security of sensitive healthcare information. Organizations that handle protected health information (PHI), including hospitals, clinics, insurers, and third-party service providers, must comply with HIPAA regulations to ensure that patient data remains confidential, secure, and accessible only to authorized individuals. Identity and Access Management (IAM) plays a crucial role in HIPAA compliance by enforcing access controls, authentication mechanisms, and audit logging to safeguard healthcare data. Without a properly structured IAM framework, organizations risk non-compliance, which can lead to substantial fines, legal consequences, and reputational damage.

HIPAA mandates strict access control measures to ensure that only authorized personnel can access PHI. The principle of least privilege is a fundamental requirement, meaning that employees, contractors, and third-party vendors should only be granted the minimum level of access necessary to perform their duties. IAM solutions enforce this principle by implementing role-based access control (RBAC) and attribute-based access control (ABAC), ensuring that permissions are granted based on job responsibilities and predefined policies. By limiting unnecessary access to PHI, organizations reduce the risk of data breaches and unauthorized disclosures.

Authentication and identity verification are critical components of HIPAA compliance. The law requires organizations to implement strong authentication mechanisms to verify user identities before granting access to PHI. Multi-factor authentication (MFA) enhances security by requiring users to provide multiple forms of verification, such as a password, biometric scan, or security token. Password policies must also be enforced to prevent weak or compromised credentials from being exploited by attackers. IAM solutions help organizations manage authentication policies, ensuring that access to healthcare systems is secure and compliant with HIPAA standards.

Auditability and logging are essential for demonstrating HIPAA compliance. Organizations must maintain comprehensive records of access to PHI, including user login attempts, data access activities, and privilege escalations. These audit logs provide a transparent record of who accessed patient data, when it was accessed, and what actions were performed. IAM solutions integrate with Security Information and Event Management (SIEM) systems to centralize access logs, enabling real-time monitoring and anomaly detection. Regular audits help organizations identify potential security risks, investigate suspicious activities, and provide documentation for regulatory inspections.

The enforcement of automatic session timeouts is another IAM best practice that aligns with HIPAA requirements. Healthcare professionals often work in fast-paced environments where they may leave their workstations unattended. If an authenticated session remains open, unauthorized individuals could access PHI. IAM solutions enforce session timeout policies that automatically log users out after a period of inactivity, reducing the risk of unauthorized access. Additionally, organizations must implement workstation locking policies to require reauthentication when users return to their devices.

Healthcare organizations frequently rely on third-party vendors and service providers who require access to patient data. HIPAA mandates that covered entities ensure that business associates implement appropriate security measures to protect PHI. IAM solutions help organizations manage third-party access by enforcing just-in-time (JIT) provisioning, granting temporary access only when necessary, and revoking access once tasks are completed. Third-party accounts should be subject to the same authentication and auditing requirements as internal users to prevent security gaps and compliance violations.

Identity lifecycle management is crucial for maintaining HIPAA compliance. Organizations must implement processes to provision, modify, and deprovision user accounts as employees join, move within, or leave the organization. When a healthcare worker changes roles or departs, their access must be promptly updated or revoked to prevent unauthorized access to PHI. IAM solutions automate these processes by integrating with human resources (HR) systems, ensuring that access rights align with employment status and job responsibilities. Failing to properly manage identity lifecycles can result in former employees retaining access to critical systems, increasing the risk of data breaches.

Emergency access protocols, also known as break-glass procedures, are required under HIPAA to ensure that healthcare providers can access PHI during urgent situations. IAM solutions facilitate secure emergency access by granting temporary elevated privileges under controlled conditions. These access events must be closely monitored and logged to ensure compliance. Organizations should implement safeguards that prevent abuse of emergency access privileges while allowing healthcare professionals to access critical patient data when necessary.

Data encryption is another essential IAM best practice for HIPAA compliance. The regulation requires organizations to protect PHI both in transit and at rest. IAM solutions help enforce encryption policies by integrating with secure authentication and access control mechanisms. Strong encryption ensures that even if unauthorized individuals gain access to stored data or intercepted communications, the information remains unreadable. Organizations must also enforce encryption for remote access, mobile devices, and cloud-based healthcare applications to maintain HIPAA compliance.

Regular security training and awareness programs are necessary to ensure that employees understand IAM policies and HIPAA compliance requirements. Human error remains one of the leading causes of data breaches in healthcare. IAM solutions can reinforce security training by prompting users to review compliance policies during login, enforcing security reminders, and requiring periodic security assessments. Educating employees on proper access management practices reduces the risk of accidental data exposure and enhances overall security awareness within the organization.

IAM automation streamlines compliance efforts by reducing manual intervention in access management processes. Automated access provisioning and deprovisioning reduce the likelihood of human errors that can lead to security gaps. IAM solutions can generate compliance reports, track policy violations, and provide real-time visibility into access control enforcement. By leveraging automation, organizations improve efficiency, accuracy, and adherence to HIPAA requirements.

Failing to comply with HIPAA regulations can result in severe financial penalties, legal consequences, and loss of patient trust. Security breaches involving PHI can lead to significant reputational damage and regulatory investigations. By implementing IAM best practices, healthcare organizations can mitigate risks, strengthen security, and ensure compliance with HIPAA requirements. IAM serves as the foundation for protecting patient data, preventing unauthorized access, and maintaining the integrity of healthcare systems.

NIST Guidelines for IAM Audit and Security

The National Institute of Standards and Technology (NIST) provides comprehensive guidelines for Identity and Access Management (IAM) audit and security, helping organizations establish best practices for securing digital identities, managing access control, and ensuring compliance with regulatory requirements. These guidelines serve as a foundation for organizations operating in both the public and private sectors, offering a structured approach to identity governance, authentication, authorization, and continuous monitoring. By following NIST recommendations, organizations can strengthen their IAM strategies, mitigate security risks, and ensure that access to critical systems and data is properly managed and audited.

NIST Special Publication 800-53 outlines security and privacy controls for federal information systems and organizations, including IAM-related requirements. It emphasizes the importance of identity proofing, authentication mechanisms, role-based access control, and privileged account management. Organizations must verify the identity of users before granting access to systems, ensuring that only authorized individuals can interact with sensitive data. Identity proofing involves validating user credentials through reliable sources, reducing the risk of identity fraud and unauthorized access. Multi-factor authentication (MFA) is a key requirement in NIST guidelines, strengthening security by requiring users to provide multiple forms of verification before accessing critical resources.

Access control is a fundamental principle in NIST's IAM framework. The guidelines recommend implementing least privilege access, ensuring that users receive only the minimum permissions necessary to perform their tasks. Role-based access control (RBAC) and attribute-based access control (ABAC) are widely used models to enforce this principle, helping organizations restrict access based on predefined rules and contextual attributes such as job role, department, location, and risk level. Privileged access management (PAM) is another critical area covered by NIST, requiring organizations to implement strict controls over privileged accounts to prevent misuse, insider threats, and unauthorized escalations of privilege.

Auditing and continuous monitoring are essential components of NIST's IAM security framework. Organizations must establish logging mechanisms to track user access, authentication attempts, system changes, and security events. These logs serve as a valuable resource for detecting suspicious activities, investigating incidents, and demonstrating compliance with security policies. NIST guidelines emphasize the need for Security Information and Event Management (SIEM) systems to centralize, analyze, and correlate access logs in real time. By leveraging automated logging and monitoring solutions, organizations can proactively identify anomalies, enforce security policies, and respond swiftly to potential threats.

NIST also highlights the importance of identity lifecycle management, requiring organizations to implement structured processes for provisioning, modifying, and deprovisioning user accounts. When employees join an organization, IAM systems must ensure that access rights are assigned based on predefined policies, reducing the risk of excessive permissions. As employees change roles or leave the organization, access must be adjusted or revoked promptly to prevent unauthorized access. Automating identity lifecycle management helps enforce security policies consistently, ensuring that inactive or orphaned accounts do not become security vulnerabilities.

Authentication and authorization mechanisms must be continuously evaluated and strengthened to align with NIST recommendations. Password-based authentication alone is insufficient in today's threat landscape, requiring organizations to adopt stronger authentication methods such as biometrics, cryptographic authentication, and behavioral-based authentication. NIST guidelines encourage the adoption of risk-based authentication, where access requests are evaluated based on user behavior, location, device, and historical access patterns. If an access attempt exhibits unusual characteristics, additional verification measures can be triggered to ensure security before granting access.

The concept of zero trust architecture is reinforced in NIST's IAM security framework. Traditional perimeter-based security models are no longer sufficient in protecting modern IT environments, where users and devices operate across multiple locations and cloud services. NIST recommends implementing a zero trust approach, where trust is never assumed, and continuous verification is required for every access request. Organizations must enforce strong identity verification, dynamic access controls, and continuous monitoring to detect and mitigate security risks effectively.

Federated identity management is another area covered in NIST guidelines, allowing organizations to enable secure access across multiple systems and platforms without requiring users to maintain separate credentials for each service. By implementing federated identity solutions based on standards such as Security Assertion Markup Language (SAML) and OpenID Connect (OIDC), organizations can enhance user experience, improve security, and streamline access management. NIST also emphasizes the importance of Single Sign-On (SSO) solutions, reducing password fatigue and minimizing security risks associated with weak or reused credentials.

Incident response and IAM security go hand in hand in NIST's recommendations. Organizations must establish clear procedures for responding to identity-related security incidents, such as compromised accounts, unauthorized access attempts, and credential breaches. IAM systems should be integrated with incident response tools, enabling automated detection, containment, and remediation of security threats. Organizations must also conduct regular IAM security assessments, penetration testing, and access reviews to ensure that security controls remain effective and aligned with evolving threats.

Third-party access management is a crucial aspect of NIST's IAM security guidelines. Many organizations rely on external vendors, contractors, and partners who require access to internal systems and data. NIST recommends enforcing strict access controls for third-party users, implementing just-in-time (JIT) access provisioning, and conducting regular access audits to ensure compliance with security policies. Organizations must also establish contractual agreements with third-party entities, ensuring that they adhere to IAM security standards and follow best practices for protecting sensitive information.

Training and awareness programs are essential for maintaining IAM security and compliance with NIST guidelines. Employees must be educated on security best practices, phishing threats, password hygiene, and safe authentication methods. IAM solutions can support training initiatives by enforcing security policies, displaying security reminders during login sessions, and requiring periodic compliance acknowledgments. Strengthening security awareness among employees reduces the likelihood of human errors that could compromise IAM security.

NIST's guidelines for IAM audit and security provide a comprehensive framework for organizations to enhance identity governance, strengthen access controls, and mitigate security risks. By implementing these best practices, organizations can improve their security posture, comply with regulatory requirements, and protect sensitive data from unauthorized access. IAM serves as the backbone of cybersecurity, ensuring that identities are managed securely, access is granted appropriately, and security events are monitored and addressed in real time.

ISO 27001 Standards for Identity and Access Controls

ISO 27001 is an internationally recognized standard for information security management systems (ISMS), providing a framework for organizations to protect sensitive data, manage risks, and ensure compliance with security best practices. Identity and Access Management (IAM) plays a critical role in ISO 27001 compliance by establishing controls that govern how identities are managed, how access to systems and data is granted, and how authentication mechanisms are enforced. Effective implementation of IAM controls aligned with ISO 27001 helps organizations strengthen security, prevent unauthorized access, and maintain accountability over sensitive information assets.

ISO 27001 emphasizes the importance of access control policies to regulate how users interact with information systems. Organizations must define and document clear policies that outline how access to systems, applications, and data is granted, modified, and revoked. These policies must be based on business needs, risk assessments, and compliance requirements. Access control policies should specify who can access what resources, under what conditions, and with what level of privilege. IAM solutions help enforce these policies by automating access provisioning, ensuring that permissions are granted based on predefined rules, and preventing excessive or inappropriate access rights.

The standard also requires organizations to implement the principle of least privilege, ensuring that users have only the minimum level of access necessary to perform their job functions. Role-based access control (RBAC) and attribute-based access control (ABAC) are commonly used approaches to enforce this principle. RBAC assigns permissions based on job roles, ensuring that users with similar responsibilities receive standardized access rights. ABAC considers additional attributes such as department, location, or risk level to provide more granular control. By enforcing least privilege access, organizations reduce the risk of data breaches caused by excessive permissions or insider threats.

Authentication mechanisms are a fundamental requirement of ISO 27001's access control standards. Organizations must establish secure authentication processes to verify user identities before granting access to information systems. Multi-factor authentication (MFA) is recommended to enhance security by requiring multiple forms of verification, such as passwords, biometrics, security tokens, or smart cards. Password management policies must also be enforced, requiring users to create strong passwords, change them regularly, and avoid reuse. IAM solutions help enforce authentication policies consistently, reducing the risk of unauthorized access due to weak or compromised credentials.

User access reviews and recertification processes are essential to maintaining compliance with ISO 27001. Organizations must regularly review user access rights to ensure that permissions remain appropriate and aligned with job responsibilities. Automated IAM solutions streamline the recertification process by generating reports on user access, identifying inactive accounts, and highlighting potential security risks. Conducting periodic access reviews helps organizations detect anomalies, revoke unnecessary privileges, and prevent the accumulation of excessive access rights over time.

ISO 27001 requires organizations to implement logging and monitoring mechanisms to track access activities and detect security incidents. IAM systems must generate detailed logs of user authentication attempts, access requests, privilege escalations, and system changes. These logs must be securely stored, protected from tampering, and regularly reviewed for suspicious activity. Security Information and Event Management (SIEM) solutions can integrate with IAM logs to provide real-time analysis, enabling organizations to identify security threats and respond proactively. Auditable access logs are also crucial for demonstrating compliance during ISO 27001 certification assessments.

Privileged access management (PAM) is another critical control under ISO 27001. Privileged accounts, such as system administrators, database administrators, and security analysts, have elevated permissions that can pose significant security risks if misused. Organizations must implement strict controls over privileged access, including just-in-time access provisioning, session recording, and approval workflows for privilege escalations. PAM solutions help enforce these controls by ensuring that privileged access is granted only when necessary and that all privileged activities are logged for accountability.

Identity lifecycle management is an essential aspect of IAM compliance with ISO 27001. Organizations must establish standardized processes for provisioning, modifying, and deprovisioning user accounts. When employees join an organization, their access rights should be granted based on predefined access policies, ensuring that they receive the appropriate permissions without excessive privileges. When employees change roles, their access must be updated to reflect their new responsibilities. When employees leave the organization, their access must be revoked promptly to prevent security risks associated with orphaned accounts. Automating identity lifecycle management reduces the likelihood of access control gaps and improves compliance.

ISO 27001 also requires organizations to manage third-party access securely. Many organizations rely on external vendors, contractors, and service providers who need access to internal systems and data. IAM solutions help manage third-party access by enforcing strict authentication, granting access on a need-to-know basis, and implementing time-limited access permissions. Organizations should also conduct periodic audits of third-party access to ensure compliance with security policies and contractual agreements. Establishing clear agreements with third-party entities regarding security expectations and access restrictions is crucial for reducing risks associated with external access.

The principle of segregation of duties (SoD) is another key requirement of ISO 27001's IAM standards. SoD ensures that no single user has excessive control over critical systems or processes, reducing the risk of fraud and unauthorized modifications. For example, an employee responsible for processing financial transactions should not have the ability to approve those transactions. IAM solutions help enforce SoD by defining access policies that prevent conflicting permissions and triggering alerts when violations occur. Conducting regular SoD reviews ensures that access policies remain effective and aligned with security objectives.

Incident response and IAM security integration are essential for ISO 27001 compliance. Organizations must establish clear procedures for responding to security incidents related to identity and access management. IAM solutions should integrate with incident response tools to provide automated detection, containment, and remediation of security threats. If an unauthorized access attempt is detected, IAM systems should trigger alerts, revoke access, and enforce additional verification measures. Organizations should also conduct regular security assessments, penetration testing, and IAM audits to identify vulnerabilities and strengthen security controls.

Employee training and awareness programs are vital for maintaining compliance with ISO 27001's IAM requirements. Users must be educated on access control policies, password security, phishing risks, and best practices for protecting sensitive information. IAM solutions can support training initiatives by enforcing policy acknowledgments, displaying security reminders, and requiring periodic security awareness assessments. Strengthening security awareness among employees helps reduce the likelihood of human errors that could compromise IAM security.

ISO 27001 provides a structured framework for organizations to establish and maintain effective IAM security controls. By implementing access control policies, enforcing authentication mechanisms, conducting regular access reviews, and integrating IAM with security monitoring tools, organizations can achieve compliance with ISO 27001 while enhancing their overall security posture. IAM serves as the foundation for protecting sensitive information, ensuring accountability, and mitigating security risks across the organization.

Identity Governance and Administration (IGA) in Compliance

Identity Governance and Administration (IGA) is a critical component of compliance in Identity and Access Management (IAM), ensuring that organizations maintain control over user identities, access privileges, and security policies. As regulatory frameworks such as SOX, GDPR, HIPAA, NIST, and ISO 27001 impose strict requirements on how organizations manage access to sensitive data, IGA provides a structured approach to enforcing compliance, minimizing risks, and enhancing security. By implementing IGA effectively, organizations can automate identity management processes, enforce least privilege access, conduct regular access reviews, and maintain an auditable record of identity-related activities.

One of the fundamental aspects of IGA in compliance is identity lifecycle management. Organizations must establish well-defined processes for provisioning, modifying, and deprovisioning user accounts based on job roles and responsibilities. When an employee joins an organization, their access should be granted according to predefined policies, ensuring that they only receive the permissions necessary for their role. As employees change positions, their access rights should be adjusted to reflect their new responsibilities, preventing them from accumulating excessive or conflicting privileges. When employees leave the organization, their access must be revoked immediately to prevent unauthorized access. Automating these processes through IGA solutions ensures consistency, reduces human error, and strengthens compliance with regulatory requirements.

Role-based access control (RBAC) and attribute-based access control (ABAC) are essential frameworks within IGA that help organizations enforce the principle of least privilege. RBAC assigns permissions based on predefined job roles, ensuring that employees only have access to the resources they need. ABAC introduces additional contextual attributes, such as location, time of access, and risk level, to refine access controls further. By implementing these models, organizations can prevent excessive access privileges, reduce security risks, and demonstrate compliance with regulations that mandate strict access controls.

Access certification and periodic reviews are key components of IGA that support compliance. Regulatory requirements such as SOX, GDPR, and HIPAA mandate that organizations conduct regular access reviews to validate that users have appropriate permissions. Access certification processes involve reviewing user access rights, identifying anomalies, and revoking unnecessary privileges. Automated IGA solutions streamline this process by generating reports, alerting managers to access discrepancies, and enforcing corrective actions. Regular access reviews help organizations maintain compliance, detect potential security risks, and ensure that employees do not retain unauthorized access to critical systems.

Auditability and reporting are crucial for demonstrating compliance with regulatory standards. Organizations must maintain a clear record of identity-related activities, including user provisioning, role assignments, access approvals, and privilege modifications. IGA solutions provide centralized logging and reporting capabilities, allowing organizations to generate compliance reports, track policy violations, and present audit trails to regulatory authorities. Security Information and Event Management (SIEM) systems can integrate with IGA platforms to analyze identity-related data in real time, detecting unauthorized access attempts, suspicious privilege escalations, and compliance violations. Maintaining detailed logs and audit trails ensures that organizations can provide evidence of adherence to regulatory requirements and respond effectively to security incidents.

Separation of duties (SoD) is a critical governance control that IGA enforces to prevent conflicts of interest and reduce fraud risks. Many regulations, including SOX and ISO 27001, require organizations to implement SoD policies that prevent users from holding conflicting permissions. For example, an employee responsible for initiating financial transactions should not have the authority to approve them.

IGA solutions help organizations define and enforce SoD policies by identifying conflicting access rights, issuing alerts for violations, and restricting access based on predefined rules. Enforcing SoD ensures that access privileges are assigned in a way that prevents fraud, strengthens compliance, and enhances security.

Privileged access management (PAM) is closely related to IGA and plays a crucial role in compliance. Privileged accounts, such as system administrators and database managers, have elevated permissions that pose significant security risks if misused. IGA solutions help organizations manage privileged accounts by enforcing strict approval workflows, implementing just-in-time (JIT) access provisioning, and logging all privileged activities. By integrating PAM with IGA, organizations can maintain control over privileged identities, reduce insider threats, and ensure that privileged access is granted only when necessary and properly monitored.

Third-party identity governance is an essential aspect of IGA compliance, as organizations frequently grant access to external vendors, contractors, and business partners. Regulatory requirements demand that organizations ensure third-party users follow the same security controls as internal employees. IGA solutions help manage third-party access by enforcing authentication policies, applying temporary access restrictions, and conducting regular access audits. Organizations must also establish contractual agreements with third-party entities, outlining security expectations, compliance requirements, and access termination procedures. Managing third-party identities effectively reduces risks associated with supply chain attacks and ensures compliance with security regulations.

Self-service identity management is another component of IGA that improves compliance while enhancing user efficiency. Organizations can implement self-service portals that allow employees to request access, reset passwords, and review their own permissions. These self-service capabilities reduce administrative workload, improve user experience, and enforce access request approval workflows. IGA solutions ensure that all self-service access requests are documented, reviewed, and approved based on compliance policies. Enabling self-service identity management strengthens security by eliminating manual processes prone to errors and inconsistencies.

Incident response and identity governance integration ensure that organizations can detect and mitigate identity-related security threats. Regulatory requirements such as GDPR and NIST emphasize the need for organizations to have structured incident response plans for identity breaches. IGA solutions integrate with security monitoring tools to detect unauthorized access, trigger automated alerts, and initiate remediation actions. If an account is compromised, IGA platforms can enforce immediate access revocation, reset authentication credentials, and generate incident reports. A proactive approach to identity-related security incidents minimizes regulatory risks and enhances overall security resilience.

Training and awareness programs support the effectiveness of IGA by ensuring that employees understand identity governance policies and compliance obligations. Many compliance frameworks require organizations to provide regular security training to employees, helping them recognize risks associated with identity management, access control, and phishing attacks. IAM solutions reinforce training initiatives by implementing policy reminders, requiring periodic security acknowledgments, and enforcing strong authentication practices. Educating employees on identity governance best practices helps organizations maintain compliance, reduce security risks, and promote a culture of security awareness.

IGA serves as the foundation of compliance-driven identity management, enabling organizations to implement structured access controls, enforce security policies, and maintain an auditable record of identity activities. By automating identity lifecycle management, enforcing least privilege access, conducting regular access reviews, and integrating with security monitoring tools, organizations can achieve compliance with regulatory frameworks while reducing security risks. Effective IGA implementation not only ensures adherence to compliance requirements but also strengthens cybersecurity, enhances operational efficiency, and builds trust with stakeholders.

Role-Based Access Control (RBAC) and Compliance

Role-Based Access Control (RBAC) is a widely adopted framework for managing user permissions within an organization. It ensures that access to systems, applications, and data is assigned based on predefined job roles, reducing the risk of excessive or inappropriate access privileges. By implementing RBAC, organizations can enforce security policies, improve operational efficiency, and meet regulatory compliance requirements. Various compliance frameworks, including SOX, GDPR, HIPAA, NIST, and ISO 27001, mandate strict access control measures, making RBAC an essential component of an organization's identity and access management (IAM) strategy.

RBAC operates by defining roles that correspond to specific job functions and assigning access rights based on those roles. Instead of granting permissions to individual users, organizations assign them to roles, ensuring consistency and reducing administrative overhead. For example, a healthcare organization can define roles such as "Doctor," "Nurse," and "Administrator," each with specific permissions to access electronic health records (EHR), patient data, or administrative functions. This structured approach simplifies access management, minimizes human errors, and ensures compliance with regulatory requirements that mandate least privilege access.

The principle of least privilege is a fundamental security concept that RBAC enforces. It ensures that users receive only the permissions necessary to perform their tasks and nothing more. Excessive privileges increase the risk of insider threats, accidental data exposure, and compliance violations. Regulations such as SOX require strict access controls to prevent unauthorized modifications to financial records, while HIPAA mandates that healthcare providers implement measures to protect patient data. RBAC helps organizations meet these requirements by restricting access based on job roles, ensuring that users cannot exceed their authorized privileges.

RBAC also enhances accountability by providing clear visibility into who has access to what resources. Many compliance frameworks require organizations to track and audit access to sensitive data. RBAC enables organizations to generate detailed reports on user access, identifying which roles have permissions to critical systems and data. By maintaining access logs and enforcing RBAC policies, organizations can demonstrate compliance with regulatory requirements and respond effectively to audit requests. The ability to produce audit trails is essential for meeting the transparency and accountability standards set by frameworks such as GDPR and ISO 27001.

Access certification and periodic reviews are critical components of RBAC compliance. Regulatory frameworks such as SOX and HIPAA require organizations to conduct regular access reviews to validate that permissions remain appropriate over time. RBAC simplifies this process by allowing managers to review access rights at the role level rather than individually for each user. If a user's job responsibilities change, their assigned role can be updated, automatically adjusting their permissions. This approach reduces administrative burden, ensures ongoing compliance, and prevents privilege accumulation, which can lead to security risks.

RBAC supports separation of duties (SoD), an important compliance control that prevents conflicts of interest and reduces the risk of fraud. SoD ensures that no single user has excessive control over critical business processes. For example, in financial organizations, an employee responsible for initiating transactions should not have the authority to approve them. RBAC allows organizations to define and enforce SoD policies, ensuring that conflicting roles cannot be assigned to the same user. Many regulations, including SOX and ISO 27001, mandate the implementation of SoD to safeguard financial data and operational integrity.

Privileged access management (PAM) can be integrated with RBAC to enhance security and compliance. Privileged accounts, such as system administrators and database managers, require elevated permissions that pose significant security risks if mismanaged. RBAC helps control privileged access by assigning administrative roles based on necessity and implementing approval workflows for privilege escalation. This approach ensures that privileged access is granted only when required and is continuously monitored, reducing the likelihood of unauthorized changes or data breaches. Compliance frameworks such as NIST emphasize the need for strict privileged access controls, making RBAC an essential component of a secure IAM strategy.

RBAC also improves security in cloud environments, where organizations must manage access across multiple platforms and services. Cloud providers offer RBAC capabilities that allow organizations to define access policies based on roles, ensuring that cloud resources are protected from unauthorized access. Compliance frameworks such as GDPR require organizations to implement strong access controls for cloud-based data processing, and RBAC helps meet these requirements by providing a structured approach to managing cloud access. By applying RBAC to cloud environments, organizations can maintain compliance while securing their cloud infrastructure.

Third-party access management is another area where RBAC plays a crucial role in compliance. Many organizations rely on external vendors, contractors, and partners who require access to internal systems and data. Compliance regulations demand that third-party access be strictly controlled and monitored. RBAC helps enforce access restrictions by assigning third-party users to predefined roles with limited privileges. Temporary access permissions can also be implemented using RBAC, ensuring that external users only have access for the duration of their engagement. By applying RBAC principles to third-party access, organizations can reduce security risks and maintain compliance with industry regulations.

Automating RBAC implementation through IAM solutions enhances efficiency and ensures compliance with regulatory standards. Manually assigning and revoking permissions can be time-consuming and error-prone. IAM platforms allow organizations to automate role assignments based on predefined policies, reducing the risk of human error and ensuring that access rights are granted and revoked in accordance with compliance requirements. Automation also enables organizations to enforce real-time access policies, respond quickly to security threats, and maintain accurate records of user permissions. By leveraging IAM automation, organizations can strengthen security, reduce administrative workload, and ensure continuous compliance with access control regulations.

Employee training and awareness programs complement RBAC implementation by ensuring that users understand access control policies and compliance requirements. Many compliance frameworks mandate that organizations provide regular security training to employees. RBAC enforcement is most effective when users are educated on the importance of access restrictions, password security, and best practices for handling sensitive data. IAM solutions can support training initiatives by displaying policy reminders during login sessions, requiring periodic compliance acknowledgments, and enforcing security awareness assessments. Educating employees on RBAC and compliance enhances security posture and reduces the risk of access-related security incidents.

RBAC provides a structured and scalable approach to managing user access while ensuring compliance with regulatory frameworks. By enforcing least privilege access, implementing separation of duties, integrating privileged access controls, and automating role assignments, organizations can strengthen security, reduce risk exposure, and meet compliance requirements. RBAC not only simplifies access management but also provides the transparency, accountability, and auditability required for regulatory compliance.

Attribute-Based Access Control (ABAC) and Compliance

Attribute-Based Access Control (ABAC) is a dynamic and flexible access control model that grants or denies access based on a combination of attributes associated with the user, resource, action, and environment. Unlike Role-Based Access Control (RBAC), which relies solely on predefined roles, ABAC evaluates a set of policies that take into account multiple attributes such as user department, job title, location, time of access, device type, and data sensitivity. This approach enables organizations to enforce fine-grained access controls that align with compliance requirements set forth by regulations such as SOX, GDPR, HIPAA, NIST, and ISO 27001. By implementing ABAC, organizations can strengthen security, reduce the risk of unauthorized access, and ensure that access decisions are contextually appropriate.

Regulatory frameworks emphasize the importance of enforcing least privilege access to protect sensitive data and systems. ABAC enhances this principle by enabling organizations to apply granular access restrictions based on real-time contextual factors. For example, a healthcare professional may be allowed to access patient records only during business hours and only from a hospital-issued device. Similarly, financial auditors may be restricted from viewing certain financial records unless they are physically present in a secure office location. These dynamic access controls help organizations comply with strict data protection regulations by preventing unauthorized access based on changing conditions.

GDPR mandates that organizations implement appropriate security measures to protect personal data and ensure that only authorized individuals can access it. ABAC supports GDPR compliance by allowing organizations to enforce data access policies based on user attributes and the sensitivity of the information. For example, an organization can configure policies that restrict access to customer personal data unless the user has completed specific training on GDPR requirements. Additionally, ABAC enables organizations to enforce data residency policies, ensuring that data remains accessible only from approved geographic locations, a critical requirement under GDPR's cross-border data transfer regulations.

HIPAA compliance requires organizations to implement strict access controls to safeguard protected health information (PHI). ABAC enables healthcare organizations to enforce access rules that account for the role of the user, the type of medical record being accessed, and the circumstances of the access request. For example, a doctor may be granted access to a patient's medical history, but only if they are actively treating that patient. Nurses may have limited access to certain test results, while administrative staff may be restricted from viewing any clinical information. ABAC ensures that access decisions are based on policy-driven rules that align with HIPAA's security and privacy requirements.

SOX regulations require organizations to implement controls that protect financial data from unauthorized modifications and ensure data integrity. ABAC helps organizations comply with SOX by enforcing access controls based on job functions, transaction risk levels, and audit requirements. For example, an employee responsible for processing financial transactions may be required to receive explicit approval from a senior manager before accessing certain financial reports. Additionally, ABAC can restrict access to sensitive financial systems based on risk-based factors, such as login attempts from unusual geographic locations or unrecognized devices. By implementing ABAC, organizations can prevent unauthorized financial data manipulation and ensure auditability of access requests.

NIST guidelines emphasize the importance of access control mechanisms that adapt to changing security conditions. ABAC aligns with NIST's recommendations by enabling real-time access decisions that take into account risk-based attributes. For example, a government contractor accessing classified data may be required to authenticate using multi-factor authentication (MFA) and must be physically present at a secure location before access is granted. Additionally, ABAC policies can be configured to enforce security classification rules, ensuring that users with a lower security clearance cannot access highly sensitive information. The flexibility of ABAC ensures that access control policies remain adaptable to evolving security threats and regulatory changes.

ISO 27001 requires organizations to implement strict access control measures as part of their information security management system (ISMS). ABAC supports ISO 27001 compliance by allowing organizations to define access policies that align with risk management principles. For example, an organization may enforce time-based access restrictions, ensuring that certain critical systems can only be accessed during scheduled maintenance windows. ABAC also enables organizations to implement least privilege access dynamically, ensuring that users receive temporary access based on their immediate needs rather than permanent access that could be exploited. By enforcing context-aware access controls, organizations can strengthen their overall security posture and maintain compliance with ISO 27001 standards.

ABAC enhances compliance by enabling automation in access control enforcement. Traditional access management models require manual intervention to update access permissions, leading to potential human errors and security gaps. ABAC solutions integrate with identity governance platforms, ensuring that access decisions are made based on real-time policies without requiring constant administrative oversight. For example, when an employee's job role changes, their access permissions can automatically update based on predefined attribute-based policies, eliminating the need for manual adjustments. This level of automation reduces administrative overhead, improves accuracy in access management, and ensures continuous compliance with regulatory requirements.

Organizations must also ensure that ABAC policies are continuously reviewed and updated to align with evolving compliance regulations. Regulatory frameworks require organizations to conduct regular access reviews to validate that permissions remain appropriate over time. ABAC simplifies this process by providing a centralized policy engine that allows security teams to modify access rules based on new compliance mandates. By integrating ABAC with security information and event management (SIEM) tools, organizations can gain visibility into access patterns, detect anomalies, and generate compliance reports that demonstrate adherence to regulatory standards.

Incident response and risk mitigation are also enhanced through ABAC implementation. In the event of a security breach or policy violation, ABAC solutions can automatically revoke access, initiate alert notifications, and enforce temporary lockdown measures. For example, if an unauthorized login attempt is detected from a high-risk location, ABAC policies can immediately deny access and require additional identity verification steps. This proactive approach to security aligns with regulatory expectations that organizations must have incident response mechanisms in place to mitigate access-related threats. By incorporating ABAC into an organization's IAM strategy, security teams can enforce dynamic security controls while maintaining compliance with industry regulations.

ABAC provides a flexible and scalable approach to managing access control in compliance-driven environments. By leveraging attribute-based policies, organizations can implement precise access restrictions that align with regulatory requirements, security best practices, and operational needs. Whether ensuring GDPR data protection, enforcing HIPAA privacy rules, securing SOX financial systems, or adhering to NIST and ISO 27001 access control standards, ABAC enables organizations to maintain compliance while strengthening security. The ability to make real-time access decisions based on user attributes, environmental conditions, and risk factors makes ABAC an essential component of modern access control frameworks.

Multi-Factor Authentication (MFA) and Compliance Requirements

Multi-Factor Authentication (MFA) has become a fundamental requirement for securing access to critical systems, data, and applications. As cyber threats continue to evolve, regulatory frameworks such as SOX, GDPR, HIPAA, NIST, and ISO 27001 mandate the implementation of strong authentication mechanisms to prevent unauthorized access. MFA enhances security by requiring users to verify their identity using multiple authentication factors before gaining access. This approach significantly reduces the risk of credential-based attacks, such as phishing, password theft, and brute force attacks, while ensuring compliance with industry regulations.

MFA operates by combining at least two of the following authentication factors: something the user knows (password or PIN), something the user has (security token, smart card, or mobile authentication app), and something the user is (biometric data such as fingerprint, facial recognition, or retina scan). By requiring multiple verification methods, MFA ensures that even if one authentication factor is compromised, unauthorized access remains unlikely. Compliance regulations emphasize the importance of MFA in securing sensitive data, preventing identity fraud, and ensuring accountability in access control.

The Sarbanes-Oxley Act (SOX) requires organizations to implement strong access controls to protect financial data from unauthorized modification and fraudulent activities. MFA helps organizations comply with SOX by ensuring that only authorized users can access financial reporting systems, accounting databases, and other critical financial assets. Implementing MFA in financial environments prevents unauthorized login attempts and strengthens auditability by providing clear authentication logs. Organizations can use MFA logs to demonstrate compliance with SOX requirements, proving that access control measures are in place to prevent unauthorized changes to financial records.

The General Data Protection Regulation (GDPR) mandates strict data protection measures to safeguard personal information. MFA supports GDPR compliance by preventing unauthorized access to systems that store or process personal data. If an organization experiences a data breach due to weak authentication, it may face significant fines under GDPR. MFA mitigates this risk by ensuring that only legitimate users can access sensitive information, reducing the likelihood of unauthorized data exposure. Additionally, MFA provides organizations with the ability to enforce conditional access policies, granting or denying access based on the authentication factors presented. By implementing MFA, organizations can demonstrate their commitment to GDPR's security and privacy requirements.

The Health Insurance Portability and Accountability Act (HIPAA) requires healthcare organizations to protect electronic protected health information (ePHI) by implementing strict access controls. MFA plays a crucial role in securing healthcare records by preventing unauthorized individuals from accessing patient data. Hospitals, clinics, and healthcare providers must enforce MFA for doctors, nurses, and administrative staff who access medical records, prescribing systems, and billing information. HIPAA audits often review authentication controls to ensure compliance, and organizations that fail to implement MFA may face penalties for failing to secure patient information adequately. By deploying MFA in healthcare environments, organizations enhance security, reduce the risk of insider threats, and ensure that only authorized personnel can access sensitive health data.

The National Institute of Standards and Technology (NIST) provides guidelines for authentication and access control, recommending the use of MFA to protect digital identities. NIST Special Publication 800-63 outlines best practices for implementing secure authentication mechanisms, emphasizing the importance of strong, adaptive authentication models. Organizations following NIST guidelines must ensure that MFA is used for accessing high-risk systems, cloud environments, and remote access platforms. NIST encourages organizations to use modern authentication methods such as passwordless authentication, adaptive MFA, and biometric verification to enhance security. By aligning MFA policies with NIST recommendations, organizations can meet compliance standards while strengthening their overall security posture.

ISO 27001, an international standard for information security management systems (ISMS), requires organizations to implement strong authentication controls to protect sensitive data. MFA supports ISO 27001 compliance by enforcing layered authentication mechanisms, ensuring that access to critical systems is restricted to authorized users. ISO 27001 also emphasizes the importance of access logging, requiring organizations to track authentication attempts, failed login attempts, and account lockout events. By integrating MFA with security monitoring tools, organizations can enhance visibility into authentication activities and detect potential security threats. Organizations pursuing ISO 27001 certification must demonstrate that authentication mechanisms, including MFA, are implemented and regularly reviewed to maintain compliance.

MFA also enhances compliance with cloud security requirements. As organizations transition to cloud-based applications and services, regulatory frameworks require them to implement strong access controls to protect cloud environments. Cloud providers such as AWS, Microsoft Azure, and Google Cloud offer built-in MFA capabilities, allowing organizations to enforce authentication policies for accessing cloud resources. Compliance standards such as GDPR and ISO 27001 require organizations to secure cloud access by implementing MFA to prevent unauthorized logins and reduce the risk of data breaches. By enabling MFA for cloud applications, organizations can protect sensitive data and meet regulatory obligations for securing cloud-based environments.

One of the challenges organizations face when implementing MFA for compliance is balancing security and user convenience. While MFA enhances security, it can also introduce friction in the authentication process, leading to user resistance. To address this challenge, organizations can implement adaptive authentication, which dynamically adjusts authentication requirements based on risk factors such as device type, location, and user behavior. For example, if a user logs in from a trusted corporate network, they may only be required to provide a password. However, if the same user attempts to log in from an unrecognized device in a foreign country, the system may enforce additional authentication factors, such as a one-time passcode or biometric verification. Adaptive MFA ensures that authentication requirements remain strong while minimizing disruptions for legitimate users.

MFA implementation must also align with compliance auditing and reporting requirements. Regulatory frameworks often require organizations to maintain records of authentication attempts, access approvals, and failed login attempts. Organizations can integrate MFA with identity governance solutions to generate compliance reports that track authentication activities, ensuring that security policies are enforced consistently. By maintaining an auditable record of MFA enforcement, organizations can demonstrate compliance with regulatory standards and provide evidence of authentication controls during security assessments.

Organizations must also establish policies for managing lost or compromised authentication factors. Regulatory frameworks require organizations to have incident response plans for handling authentication-related security incidents. If a user loses their MFA token or experiences a compromised authentication method, organizations must have procedures in place to verify the user's identity securely and issue a replacement authentication factor. Implementing self-service MFA recovery options, such as biometric authentication or security question verification, helps organizations maintain compliance while ensuring that users can regain access securely.

MFA is a critical security control that aligns with multiple compliance regulations, ensuring that access to sensitive data and systems remains secure. By implementing MFA in accordance with regulatory requirements, organizations can prevent unauthorized access, reduce the risk of credential-based attacks, and demonstrate compliance with security best practices. Strong authentication mechanisms, combined with adaptive MFA and security monitoring, provide organizations with a comprehensive approach to securing digital identities while meeting the stringent security standards imposed by compliance frameworks.

User Access Reviews and Certification Processes

User access reviews and certification processes are critical components of identity and access management (IAM), ensuring that organizations maintain proper control over who has access to systems, applications, and sensitive data. Compliance frameworks such as SOX, GDPR, HIPAA, NIST, and ISO 27001 mandate periodic access reviews to prevent unauthorized access, detect security risks, and enforce least privilege principles. By conducting regular access reviews, organizations can verify that users retain only the permissions necessary for their roles, preventing privilege accumulation and reducing the risk of insider threats.

Access reviews involve systematically evaluating user permissions across various systems and applications to confirm their appropriateness. These reviews require organizations to assess whether employees, contractors, and third-party users still need their assigned access privileges. Managers, system owners, or security administrators typically oversee access reviews, ensuring that access rights align with current job functions and compliance policies. Organizations must also consider segregation of duties (SoD) principles, ensuring that no user holds conflicting permissions that could lead to fraud or policy violations. Regularly scheduled access reviews help organizations maintain compliance with regulatory requirements while improving overall security posture.

The certification process in IAM requires decision-makers to formally approve or revoke user access based on review findings. Certification ensures that user permissions are justified and that access to critical systems is restricted to authorized individuals. This process often involves multiple stakeholders, including department managers, IT security teams, and compliance officers. Certification workflows can be automated using IAM solutions, reducing the administrative burden and improving efficiency. Automating access certification allows organizations to enforce consistent review processes, maintain audit trails, and demonstrate compliance with industry regulations.

SOX compliance requires organizations to implement strict access controls to protect financial systems and prevent fraudulent activities. Under SOX regulations, organizations must conduct periodic access reviews to verify that only authorized personnel have access to financial records and reporting systems. User access reviews ensure that employees do not retain unnecessary privileges, reducing the risk of unauthorized modifications to financial data. Auditors often examine access review reports during SOX assessments, requiring organizations to maintain detailed records of access changes, review approvals, and remediation actions. Implementing automated certification processes helps organizations streamline SOX compliance while minimizing security risks.

GDPR mandates that organizations enforce strict access controls to protect personal data from unauthorized access or exposure. User access reviews play a crucial role in GDPR compliance by ensuring that only authorized individuals can process or view personally identifiable information (PII). Organizations must review and certify user access to customer data, HR records, and other sensitive information regularly. If an employee no longer requires access to personal data, their permissions must be revoked promptly to prevent data breaches. GDPR also requires organizations to document access review findings, providing evidence that access controls are actively managed and enforced. IAM solutions enable organizations to generate compliance reports that demonstrate GDPR adherence during regulatory audits.

HIPAA compliance requires healthcare organizations to implement access controls that restrict electronic protected health information (ePHI) to authorized personnel. User access reviews help hospitals, clinics, and healthcare providers verify that employees, physicians, and contractors retain only the minimum necessary access to medical records. HIPAA regulations emphasize the importance of access certification, requiring organizations to regularly review and adjust access permissions based on job roles and responsibilities. Failure to conduct access reviews can result in compliance violations, regulatory fines, and increased risk of data breaches. Automating access reviews and certification processes enhances security and ensures that healthcare organizations remain compliant with HIPAA standards.

NIST guidelines stress the importance of continuous monitoring and access governance in cybersecurity frameworks. Regular user access reviews align with NIST best practices by ensuring that user permissions remain appropriate over time. NIST recommends that organizations integrate automated certification workflows to reduce manual errors and improve audit readiness. Organizations implementing NIST-compliant security measures must verify access rights based on risk assessments, privilege levels, and business needs. By leveraging IAM solutions, organizations can enforce NIST's recommendations, ensuring that access reviews are performed consistently and effectively.

ISO 27001 requires organizations to maintain an information security management system (ISMS) that includes strict access control policies. User access reviews are an essential part of ISO 27001 compliance, helping organizations enforce least privilege access and prevent unauthorized system access. ISO 27001 mandates that access control policies be reviewed and updated periodically to reflect changes in organizational structure, job functions, and security risks. Certification processes ensure that access reviews result in actionable decisions, such as revoking unnecessary permissions or granting temporary access based on business needs. Organizations pursuing ISO 27001 certification must demonstrate that access controls are continuously reviewed, validated, and enforced to maintain compliance.

Conducting user access reviews manually can be time-consuming and error-prone. Many organizations rely on IAM automation to streamline access certification processes and improve accuracy. IAM solutions integrate with HR systems, directory services, and security monitoring tools to provide real-time visibility into user permissions. Automated access reviews generate alerts for excessive or inactive permissions, prompting managers to take corrective action. Additionally, IAM platforms allow organizations to enforce policy-based access reviews, triggering review cycles based on predefined criteria such as employment status changes, role modifications, or high-risk access levels.

Organizations must also establish clear remediation procedures following access reviews. If a review identifies excessive privileges, orphaned accounts, or unauthorized access, immediate corrective actions must be taken. IAM solutions enable organizations to automate deprovisioning, ensuring that unnecessary access is revoked promptly. Security teams must also investigate anomalies identified during access reviews, assessing potential security risks and implementing mitigation measures. Documenting remediation actions helps organizations demonstrate compliance and improve access governance.

Third-party access reviews are essential for organizations that grant external vendors, consultants, and partners access to internal systems. Compliance frameworks require organizations to monitor and review third-party access regularly, ensuring that external users do not retain unnecessary permissions after project completion. IAM solutions facilitate third-party access certification by tracking vendor accounts, enforcing time-limited access, and requiring periodic reapproval of third-party access rights. Regular access reviews help organizations mitigate supply chain security risks while maintaining compliance with regulatory requirements.

Employee training and awareness programs support effective access review processes by ensuring that users understand compliance obligations and security policies. Organizations should educate managers on the importance of timely access reviews and certification procedures. IAM solutions can reinforce security awareness by displaying policy reminders, requiring users to acknowledge compliance guidelines, and providing self-service access request portals. Strengthening access governance through training initiatives enhances overall security while promoting compliance with access control regulations.

User access reviews and certification processes provide organizations with a structured approach to managing access control, enforcing least privilege, and meeting regulatory compliance requirements. By implementing automated access reviews, integrating certification workflows, and maintaining detailed audit records, organizations can reduce security risks, improve operational efficiency, and ensure compliance with industry standards. Access governance remains a fundamental component of IAM, enabling organizations to prevent unauthorized access, protect sensitive data, and demonstrate adherence to security regulations.

Least Privilege Principle and Compliance Enforcement

The least privilege principle is a foundational security concept in identity and access management (IAM) that ensures users, applications, and systems have only the minimum permissions necessary to perform their tasks. This principle minimizes the risk of unauthorized access, insider threats, and data breaches by restricting users from having excessive privileges that could be exploited maliciously or accidentally. Compliance frameworks such as SOX, GDPR, HIPAA, NIST, and ISO 27001 mandate the enforcement of least privilege policies to protect sensitive data and maintain security integrity. Organizations must implement structured access control policies, regular access reviews, and automated privilege management to enforce compliance and strengthen cybersecurity.

Enforcing least privilege begins with role-based access control (RBAC) and attribute-based access control (ABAC), which help organizations assign access rights based on job responsibilities and contextual attributes. RBAC ensures that users are granted permissions strictly based on their job roles, preventing them from accessing systems unrelated to their responsibilities. ABAC enhances least privilege enforcement by considering additional factors such as user location, device security posture, and risk level before granting access. By implementing these models, organizations can dynamically restrict access based on business needs while aligning with compliance requirements that emphasize minimal data exposure.

Regulatory compliance frameworks require organizations to demonstrate that they have implemented and maintained least privilege access controls. SOX mandates strict access restrictions for financial systems to prevent fraudulent activities and unauthorized financial reporting modifications. Organizations subject to SOX compliance must document their access control policies, track user permissions, and provide evidence of access reviews that ensure employees only retain necessary privileges. Least privilege enforcement helps organizations prevent financial data manipulation, reducing the risk of compliance violations and audit failures.

GDPR emphasizes the protection of personal data by requiring organizations to enforce access restrictions that limit who can view, process, or modify personally identifiable information (PII). Least privilege ensures that employees only have access to PII when it is required for their job functions. Organizations must prevent excessive data exposure by revoking unnecessary permissions and ensuring that access to customer data is tightly controlled. GDPR compliance audits often review access logs and privilege assignments to verify that organizations are adhering to least privilege policies. Failure to enforce these restrictions can result in regulatory fines and reputational damage.

HIPAA enforces strict access controls to protect electronic protected health information (ePHI) within healthcare organizations. Least privilege is a core requirement for HIPAA compliance, ensuring that healthcare providers, administrative staff, and third-party vendors only access patient data when necessary. Organizations must implement access control policies that prevent unauthorized individuals from viewing, modifying, or transmitting patient records. HIPAA regulations require regular privilege audits and access reviews to ensure that permissions remain appropriate over time. Least privilege enforcement reduces the risk of data breaches, insider threats, and accidental disclosure of patient information.

NIST guidelines advocate for the implementation of least privilege as part of a broader cybersecurity strategy. Organizations following NIST recommendations must ensure that user privileges are restricted based on risk assessments, operational needs, and security requirements. NIST's zero trust architecture model aligns with least privilege enforcement by eliminating implicit trust and continuously verifying access requests. Organizations must adopt just-in-time (JIT) privilege escalation methods, granting temporary elevated access only when required and automatically revoking it once the task is completed. By implementing NIST-recommended security measures, organizations can minimize attack surfaces and enhance compliance with access control best practices.

ISO 27001 requires organizations to establish an information security management system (ISMS) that includes strict access control policies. Least privilege enforcement ensures that employees and third-party users do not have excessive access to critical systems and data. ISO 27001 audits evaluate whether organizations have implemented access controls that align with least privilege principles. Organizations must document privilege assignments, conduct periodic access reviews, and enforce privilege reduction measures when necessary. By aligning least privilege policies with ISO 27001 standards, organizations can demonstrate compliance, reduce security risks, and maintain a strong security posture.

Privileged access management (PAM) plays a crucial role in enforcing least privilege for high-risk accounts, such as administrators and database managers. Privileged accounts have elevated permissions that can be exploited if not properly managed. Organizations must implement PAM solutions that enforce session monitoring, approval workflows for privilege escalation, and automatic privilege de-escalation once tasks are completed. Compliance regulations require organizations to control privileged access strictly, ensuring that administrative users do not retain unnecessary permissions that could lead to security breaches. PAM solutions provide detailed audit trails, enabling organizations to track privileged activities and respond to suspicious behavior in real time.

Automating least privilege enforcement reduces human error and improves compliance efficiency. Manual privilege assignment processes increase the risk of excessive access permissions, leading to security vulnerabilities. IAM solutions automate access provisioning, ensuring that users receive predefined privilege levels based on policy-driven rules. Automated privilege revocation processes remove unnecessary access when users change roles, leave the organization, or no longer require specific permissions. IAM automation enhances compliance by providing real-time visibility into privilege assignments, generating audit reports, and triggering alerts for excessive access violations.

Organizations must conduct regular access reviews to validate that least privilege policies are effectively enforced. Compliance frameworks require periodic assessments to ensure that user permissions align with job responsibilities and business needs. Automated access review workflows enable managers to evaluate and approve or revoke privileges efficiently. IAM solutions generate access certification reports that demonstrate compliance with regulatory requirements, providing auditors with clear evidence of least privilege enforcement. Regular privilege audits help organizations maintain compliance while preventing security risks associated with privilege creep.

Third-party access management is another critical aspect of least privilege enforcement. Organizations frequently grant external vendors, contractors, and business partners access to internal systems and data. Compliance frameworks mandate that third-party access be restricted based on business necessity, time limitations, and security risk assessments. Least privilege policies ensure that third-party users receive only the minimum permissions required to perform their tasks. IAM solutions facilitate third-party access controls by enforcing temporary access policies, requiring multi-factor authentication (MFA), and tracking external user activities. Restricting third-party access prevents supply chain security risks and strengthens compliance with data protection regulations.

Employee training and security awareness programs support least privilege enforcement by ensuring that users understand access control policies and compliance obligations. Organizations must educate employees on privilege restrictions, phishing risks, and secure access practices. IAM solutions reinforce security training by prompting users to acknowledge least privilege policies during authentication processes and requiring periodic security assessments. Educating employees on access management best practices helps organizations maintain compliance while reducing the risk of privilege misuse.

Least privilege enforcement is a fundamental requirement for regulatory compliance and effective cybersecurity. Organizations must implement structured access controls, automate privilege management, conduct regular privilege audits, and enforce strict third-party access policies. By aligning least privilege policies with compliance frameworks such as SOX, GDPR, HIPAA, NIST, and ISO 27001, organizations can mitigate security risks, protect sensitive data, and ensure adherence to industry regulations. Implementing least privilege as a core security principle strengthens overall IAM strategies, preventing unauthorized access while maintaining compliance integrity.

Logging and Monitoring in IAM Audits

Logging and monitoring are essential components of Identity and Access Management (IAM) audits, ensuring that organizations maintain visibility into user activities, access attempts, and security events. Compliance frameworks such as SOX, GDPR, HIPAA, NIST, and ISO 27001 require organizations to implement robust logging mechanisms and continuous monitoring to detect unauthorized access, policy violations, and potential security threats. Effective logging and monitoring enable organizations to track identity-related activities, investigate security incidents, and provide audit trails for regulatory compliance. By implementing structured logging and real-time monitoring, organizations can strengthen IAM security while meeting industry standards.

Logging in IAM audits involves capturing and storing records of authentication events, access requests, privilege escalations, and administrative actions. These logs provide a historical record of user interactions with systems, allowing security teams to analyze activity patterns and detect anomalies. Organizations must configure IAM solutions to log critical events such as successful and failed login attempts, password changes, role modifications, and access revocations. Capturing these events helps organizations identify security incidents and enforce accountability for user actions. Logs should be securely stored and protected from tampering, ensuring their integrity and availability for audit purposes.

Regulatory compliance mandates that organizations maintain detailed access logs to demonstrate adherence to security policies. SOX requires companies to track access to financial systems, ensuring that only authorized personnel can view or modify financial data. IAM logs provide auditors with evidence of access control enforcement, highlighting any unauthorized attempts to access sensitive information. Organizations must implement logging policies that align with SOX requirements, ensuring that financial system access is continuously monitored and documented. By maintaining a clear record of user activities, organizations can prevent fraudulent actions and reduce the risk of financial data manipulation.

GDPR mandates strict access controls and logging requirements to protect personal data. Organizations must document who accessed personal data, when it was accessed, and for what purpose. IAM logs support GDPR compliance by capturing access events and providing audit trails that demonstrate accountability. If a data breach occurs, GDPR requires organizations to report the incident within 72 hours, and access logs play a crucial role in identifying the cause and scope of the breach. Organizations must ensure that IAM logging systems retain records for an appropriate period, allowing regulators to verify compliance with data protection requirements. By maintaining comprehensive IAM logs, organizations can track access to personal data and respond to GDPR compliance inquiries effectively.

HIPAA requires healthcare organizations to implement logging and monitoring mechanisms to protect electronic protected health information (ePHI). IAM logs play a critical role in tracking access to patient records, ensuring that only authorized healthcare professionals can view or modify medical data. HIPAA compliance audits review IAM logs to verify that access controls are enforced, preventing unauthorized disclosure of ePHI. Healthcare organizations must configure IAM logging systems to detect suspicious access attempts, unauthorized privilege escalations, and unusual user behavior. Real-time monitoring helps security teams respond to potential HIPAA violations, reducing the risk of data breaches and regulatory fines.

NIST provides guidelines for IAM logging and monitoring, emphasizing the importance of continuous auditing to detect security threats. Organizations following NIST recommendations must implement centralized logging systems that aggregate identity-related events from multiple sources, including authentication servers, access control systems, and cloud environments. Security Information and Event Management (SIEM) solutions help organizations analyze IAM logs, correlating security events to identify potential threats. NIST recommends implementing automated alerting mechanisms that notify security teams of unusual access patterns, failed login attempts, and privilege escalation activities. By integrating IAM logging with SIEM platforms, organizations can enhance threat detection and ensure compliance with NIST security controls.

ISO 27001 requires organizations to maintain an Information Security Management System (ISMS) that includes logging and monitoring controls. IAM logs are essential for tracking access to critical systems, detecting policy violations, and ensuring compliance with ISO 27001 security standards. Organizations must implement logging mechanisms that capture access attempts, authentication failures, and administrative actions. IAM monitoring solutions should generate audit reports that provide visibility into access management trends, enabling organizations to assess security risks and enforce access control policies. ISO 27001 auditors review IAM logs to ensure that access control policies are implemented effectively and that security incidents are promptly addressed.

Real-time monitoring enhances IAM audits by enabling organizations to detect and respond to security threats as they occur. Continuous monitoring solutions analyze IAM logs in real time, identifying suspicious activities such as repeated failed login attempts, unusual access locations, and unauthorized privilege modifications. Automated response mechanisms can trigger alerts, revoke access, or enforce additional authentication requirements when anomalous behavior is detected. Organizations must implement monitoring tools that provide real-time visibility into identity-related security events, reducing the likelihood of access-related breaches.

Privileged access monitoring is a critical aspect of IAM auditing, ensuring that high-risk accounts are not misused. Privileged accounts, such as system administrators and database managers, have elevated permissions that could be exploited if not properly controlled. IAM logs must capture privileged access sessions, recording actions such as configuration changes, data modifications, and security policy updates. Organizations should implement session recording for privileged accounts, providing a forensic trail of activities performed by administrators. Compliance regulations require organizations to monitor privileged access continuously, ensuring that elevated permissions are used appropriately and that unauthorized actions are detected.

IAM logging and monitoring must also extend to cloud environments, where organizations manage access to cloud-based applications and infrastructure. Cloud service providers offer logging capabilities that capture identity-related events, including authentication attempts, access policy changes, and API interactions. Organizations must integrate cloud IAM logs with their centralized monitoring systems, ensuring that security teams have visibility into cloud access activities. Compliance frameworks require organizations to track cloud access, enforce logging retention policies, and analyze IAM logs to detect cloud-based security threats. Implementing IAM monitoring for cloud environments enhances security and ensures compliance with data protection regulations.

Third-party access logging is another critical requirement for IAM audits. Organizations often grant external vendors, contractors, and business partners access to internal systems, increasing security risks. Compliance regulations mandate that organizations track and monitor third-party access to ensure that external users do not violate security policies. IAM logs must record third-party authentication attempts, access requests, and data interactions. Continuous monitoring solutions should generate alerts for suspicious third-party activities, ensuring that security teams can respond to potential access violations. Enforcing logging and monitoring for third-party access reduces the risk of supply chain attacks and strengthens compliance efforts.

IAM audit logs must be protected against tampering and unauthorized modifications to ensure their reliability for compliance purposes. Organizations should implement secure log storage mechanisms, ensuring that logs are encrypted and access to log files is restricted. Compliance regulations require organizations to enforce log retention policies, maintaining IAM logs for a specified period to support audit investigations. Organizations must also implement integrity checks that verify the authenticity of IAM logs, ensuring that security teams can trust audit records. Protecting IAM logs from manipulation strengthens compliance efforts and provides reliable evidence of access control enforcement.

IAM logging and monitoring provide organizations with the visibility and security controls necessary to enforce compliance and protect sensitive data. By capturing access-related events, analyzing identity activities, and integrating with security monitoring tools, organizations can detect threats, investigate security incidents, and ensure compliance with industry regulations. Logging and monitoring are essential for maintaining a secure IAM environment, allowing organizations to track user activities, enforce policy compliance, and respond effectively to access-related security risks.

Audit Trails and Forensic Investigations in IAM

Audit trails are a fundamental component of Identity and Access Management (IAM), providing a chronological record of user activities, access events, and security-related actions within an organization. These trails serve as essential tools for forensic investigations, compliance audits, and security incident response. Compliance frameworks such as SOX, GDPR, HIPAA, NIST, and ISO 27001 require organizations to maintain detailed audit logs to track user access, detect unauthorized activities, and provide evidence of security policy enforcement. By implementing comprehensive audit trail mechanisms, organizations can ensure transparency, accountability, and compliance while strengthening their ability to investigate security incidents effectively.

An audit trail consists of detailed records capturing events such as user authentication attempts, privilege escalations, access approvals, data modifications, and administrative actions. These records help security teams analyze user behavior, detect anomalies, and investigate potential security breaches. Organizations must ensure that audit trails are tamper-proof, securely stored, and easily retrievable for compliance reporting and forensic analysis. IAM systems generate logs automatically, recording key details such as user identities, timestamps, access locations, and system responses to authentication requests. Centralized logging solutions help aggregate these records, ensuring that audit data is available for compliance and security monitoring.

Regulatory compliance mandates require organizations to maintain audit trails that provide visibility into access control enforcement. The Sarbanes-Oxley Act (SOX) requires organizations to document financial system access, ensuring that only authorized personnel can view or modify financial data. Audit trails help organizations track who accessed financial records, what actions were performed, and whether any unauthorized changes occurred. During a SOX audit, organizations must present logs that demonstrate compliance with security policies, ensuring that financial transactions remain transparent and verifiable. By maintaining robust audit trails, organizations can reduce fraud risks and support financial integrity.

The General Data Protection Regulation (GDPR) mandates strict logging and auditing of personal data access to ensure data protection and privacy compliance. Organizations must track when and how personally identifiable information (PII) is accessed, modified, or shared. GDPR requires organizations to document access logs and provide regulators with evidence of data protection measures in place. In the event of a data breach, forensic investigations rely on audit trails to identify the source of unauthorized access, assess the impact of the incident, and implement corrective actions. Organizations must retain audit logs for a specified period to comply with GDPR requirements and facilitate forensic investigations when necessary.

The Health Insurance Portability and Accountability Act (HIPAA) enforces strict audit trail requirements for healthcare organizations managing electronic protected health information (ePHI). Hospitals, clinics, and healthcare providers must log access to patient records, ensuring that only authorized healthcare professionals interact with medical data. Audit trails help detect unauthorized access attempts, identify insider threats, and enforce security policies that prevent data breaches. HIPAA compliance audits review access logs to verify that healthcare organizations maintain strict access controls. If a breach occurs, forensic investigations rely on audit records to determine the scope of unauthorized access and implement remediation measures.

NIST guidelines emphasize the importance of audit trails for cybersecurity incident detection and response. Organizations following NIST's security framework must implement logging mechanisms that capture user authentication attempts, privilege escalations, failed login attempts, and access denials. NIST also recommends integrating audit trails with Security Information and Event Management (SIEM) systems to analyze access patterns, detect security threats, and generate alerts for suspicious activities. During forensic investigations, security teams use audit trails to trace security incidents back to their origin, reconstruct attack vectors, and determine the impact of unauthorized access. By maintaining detailed logs, organizations enhance their ability to detect, respond to, and prevent cyber threats.

ISO 27001 requires organizations to implement an Information Security Management System (ISMS) that includes audit trail mechanisms for tracking access control enforcement. Audit logs must be retained for compliance purposes, ensuring that organizations can verify security policy adherence and detect policy violations. ISO 27001 auditors review access logs to assess whether organizations maintain sufficient audit records to support forensic investigations. Organizations must implement log retention policies that define how long audit trails are stored, ensuring that historical access records remain available for regulatory audits and security analysis.

Forensic investigations rely on audit trails to reconstruct security incidents, identify compromised accounts, and determine the scope of unauthorized activities. Security teams analyze IAM logs to detect anomalies, such as multiple failed login attempts, access from unusual geographic locations, and unauthorized privilege escalations. By correlating audit records from different systems, investigators can determine whether an attacker gained access through credential theft, exploited a vulnerability, or abused an internal user account. IAM forensic analysis helps organizations understand security incidents, mitigate ongoing threats, and prevent future attacks by strengthening access control policies.

Privileged access monitoring is a critical aspect of forensic investigations, ensuring that administrative accounts are not misused. Privileged users have elevated access to critical systems and data, making them high-value targets for attackers. Organizations must log privileged account activities, capturing details such as configuration changes, data modifications, and system updates. Audit trails help detect unusual privileged user behavior, such as unauthorized database queries or attempts to modify security settings. By continuously monitoring privileged access, organizations can prevent insider threats and quickly detect security breaches involving administrative accounts.

Tamper-proof audit trail storage is essential for maintaining the integrity and reliability of forensic evidence. Organizations must implement secure logging mechanisms that prevent unauthorized modifications to log files. Cryptographic hashing, log integrity verification, and write-once-read-many (WORM) storage solutions help protect audit trails from tampering. Compliance frameworks require organizations to implement access controls for audit logs, ensuring that only authorized personnel can review or modify logging records. Maintaining secure audit trails ensures that forensic investigations are based on trustworthy evidence, allowing organizations to respond to security incidents effectively.

Organizations must also implement real-time monitoring solutions that analyze audit logs and generate alerts for suspicious access activities. Automated monitoring tools help detect potential security incidents before they escalate, allowing security teams to investigate anomalies and take corrective actions. Forensic investigations benefit from real-time log analysis, enabling organizations to trace security breaches in progress and respond rapidly to contain threats. Continuous monitoring of audit trails enhances IAM security by providing proactive threat detection and response capabilities.

Employee training and awareness programs support effective audit trail implementation by ensuring that users understand security policies and compliance requirements. Organizations must educate employees on access control policies, logging requirements, and security best practices to reduce human errors that could compromise audit integrity. IAM solutions reinforce security awareness by displaying policy reminders, requiring users to acknowledge compliance guidelines, and enforcing security training programs. Strengthening security awareness enhances audit trail effectiveness and ensures that employees follow IAM policies that support forensic investigations.

Audit trails and forensic investigations play a critical role in IAM security, providing organizations with the visibility, accountability, and compliance enforcement necessary to protect sensitive data. By maintaining detailed access logs, implementing real-time monitoring, securing audit records, and integrating forensic analysis tools, organizations can detect security incidents, investigate access violations, and ensure compliance with industry regulations. Effective audit trail management strengthens IAM security, allowing organizations to enforce security policies, track identity-related activities, and respond to access-related threats efficiently.

Compliance Reporting and Dashboarding for IAM

Compliance reporting and dashboarding are essential components of Identity and Access Management (IAM), enabling organizations to monitor access controls, track policy violations, and demonstrate adherence to regulatory requirements. Regulations such as SOX, GDPR, HIPAA, NIST, and ISO 27001 mandate that organizations maintain accurate records of access activities and security policies. Compliance reporting provides detailed insights into IAM operations, while dashboarding offers real-time visibility into key security metrics. By implementing structured reporting mechanisms and intuitive dashboards, organizations can streamline compliance efforts, enhance security governance, and respond effectively to audit requests.

IAM compliance reporting involves generating structured reports that document user access, authentication attempts, role assignments, and privilege modifications. These reports serve as evidence that access policies are enforced and that regulatory requirements are met. Organizations must generate reports that align with specific compliance frameworks, ensuring that they capture critical identity-related events. Compliance reports must include details such as user account activity, failed login attempts, access approval workflows, and privilege escalation records. Automating compliance reporting reduces administrative overhead and ensures that audit documentation remains accurate and up to date.

Regulatory frameworks require organizations to maintain audit-ready reports that track IAM compliance status. The Sarbanes-Oxley Act (SOX) mandates that organizations document access controls for financial systems, ensuring that only authorized personnel can modify financial records. SOX compliance reports provide auditors with evidence of access governance, tracking who accessed financial systems, what actions were performed, and whether any unauthorized changes occurred. IAM solutions generate SOX compliance reports that summarize access review outcomes, role-based access policies, and privileged account usage. By automating SOX reporting, organizations can minimize audit risks and demonstrate strong access controls.

The General Data Protection Regulation (GDPR) requires organizations to maintain records of personal data access, ensuring that only authorized individuals interact with sensitive information. GDPR compliance reports document data access logs, authentication events, and security incidents related to personal data protection. Organizations must generate reports that provide transparency into identity governance, ensuring that access rights to customer data are justified and reviewed regularly. GDPR also mandates that organizations report security breaches within 72 hours, requiring accurate compliance reports that detail unauthorized access incidents. IAM compliance reporting tools help organizations maintain GDPR readiness by automating data access tracking and audit log management.

The Health Insurance Portability and Accountability Act (HIPAA) enforces strict compliance reporting requirements for healthcare organizations handling electronic protected health information (ePHI). HIPAA compliance reports document user access to medical records, authentication failures, and access approval workflows. Healthcare providers must generate reports that demonstrate compliance with role-based access control (RBAC) policies, ensuring that only authorized healthcare professionals access patient data. IAM solutions generate HIPAA audit reports that track security events, flag access anomalies, and document compliance with privacy policies. By maintaining structured HIPAA reports, healthcare organizations reduce regulatory risks and ensure that patient data remains protected.

NIST guidelines emphasize the importance of compliance reporting for access control enforcement and security monitoring. Organizations following NIST's cybersecurity framework must generate reports that track authentication trends, failed access attempts, and privilege assignment changes. NIST compliance reports provide detailed insights into IAM security posture, helping organizations detect unauthorized access and enforce least privilege policies. IAM solutions generate automated NIST compliance reports that summarize access control violations, policy enforcement trends, and security audit findings. By aligning IAM compliance reporting with NIST guidelines, organizations strengthen security governance and improve incident response capabilities.

ISO 27001 requires organizations to implement an Information Security Management System (ISMS) that includes compliance reporting for access control policies. IAM compliance reports under ISO 27001 track user authentication activities, privileged access management (PAM) events, and security incident responses. Organizations must maintain structured reports that demonstrate access control effectiveness and policy adherence. IAM solutions generate ISO 27001 compliance reports that summarize identity governance metrics, access review findings, and security audit results. By automating ISO 27001 reporting, organizations improve audit readiness and ensure continuous compliance with security standards.

IAM dashboarding provides real-time visibility into compliance metrics, enabling security teams to monitor access activities, detect policy violations, and track regulatory adherence. IAM dashboards display key compliance indicators such as failed login attempts, access certification statuses, and privilege escalation requests. Security administrators use IAM dashboards to assess compliance risks, identify security trends, and prioritize remediation efforts. Customizable dashboards allow organizations to tailor compliance monitoring based on specific regulatory requirements, ensuring that critical IAM events remain visible and actionable.

IAM dashboards integrate with security monitoring tools, providing organizations with a centralized view of identity-related security risks. Compliance dashboards display graphical representations of user activity patterns, access anomalies, and policy enforcement statistics. Organizations use IAM dashboards to track real-time security incidents, ensuring that compliance violations are detected and addressed promptly. Automated alerts notify security teams of suspicious IAM events, enabling proactive responses to potential compliance breaches. By leveraging IAM dashboarding, organizations enhance compliance monitoring and improve decision-making for access control enforcement.

Privileged access monitoring is a key feature of IAM dashboarding, allowing organizations to track administrative account activities and detect security threats. Privileged accounts have elevated permissions that pose security risks if misused. IAM dashboards display privileged session activities, identifying unauthorized privilege escalations and excessive permission grants. Security teams use privileged access dashboards to monitor high-risk accounts, ensuring that privileged users comply with access control policies. Organizations can configure IAM dashboards to generate compliance reports that summarize privileged access trends, helping auditors assess adherence to regulatory frameworks.

Third-party access reporting and dashboarding help organizations manage external vendor accounts and monitor supply chain security risks. Compliance frameworks require organizations to track third-party access permissions, ensuring that external users do not retain excessive privileges. IAM compliance reports document third-party authentication attempts, access approval workflows, and session activity logs. IAM dashboards display third-party access metrics, highlighting security risks associated with external accounts. By implementing third-party access monitoring, organizations ensure compliance with regulatory requirements and mitigate risks associated with external user privileges.

Automating compliance reporting and dashboarding improves efficiency, accuracy, and regulatory adherence. Manual reporting processes introduce inconsistencies and increase the likelihood of compliance gaps. IAM solutions generate automated compliance reports, ensuring that access control policies remain enforced and audit documentation is accurate. IAM dashboards provide security teams with real-time compliance insights, enabling organizations to address security risks proactively. By integrating compliance reporting and dashboarding with IAM frameworks, organizations strengthen identity governance, enforce regulatory requirements, and maintain comprehensive audit readiness.

Employee training and awareness programs support IAM compliance reporting by ensuring that security teams understand reporting requirements and dashboarding functionalities. Organizations must educate employees on compliance reporting standards, security policy enforcement, and IAM dashboard monitoring. IAM solutions reinforce security awareness by displaying compliance summaries, policy violation alerts, and access governance trends. Strengthening IAM compliance reporting through training initiatives enhances security oversight and ensures that organizations maintain regulatory compliance effectively.

Compliance reporting and dashboarding provide organizations with the tools needed to enforce IAM policies, track access control effectiveness, and meet regulatory requirements. By implementing automated reporting solutions and real-time dashboards, organizations enhance visibility into identity governance, improve audit readiness, and strengthen security enforcement. IAM compliance reporting ensures that organizations maintain structured access control documentation, while dashboarding enables security teams to monitor compliance trends and respond to security risks proactively.

Data Protection and Privacy Considerations in IAM

Data protection and privacy are essential components of Identity and Access Management (IAM), ensuring that sensitive information is safeguarded from unauthorized access, misuse, and breaches. Organizations must implement robust IAM policies that align with regulatory requirements such as GDPR, HIPAA, SOX, NIST, and ISO 27001 to protect personally identifiable information (PII), financial data, and other confidential assets. By integrating data protection principles with IAM, organizations can enforce strict access controls, minimize data exposure, and enhance overall security posture.

IAM plays a critical role in data protection by enforcing access control mechanisms that limit who can access specific data sets. Organizations must implement least privilege access policies to ensure that users only have permissions necessary for their job functions. Role-based access control (RBAC) and attribute-based access control (ABAC) help enforce these restrictions by assigning access based on job responsibilities, contextual attributes, and security risk assessments. Implementing these models reduces the likelihood of unauthorized access to sensitive information and strengthens compliance with data protection regulations.

Regulatory frameworks impose strict data privacy requirements that IAM must address. The General Data Protection Regulation (GDPR) mandates that organizations protect personal data by enforcing access restrictions, encryption, and logging mechanisms. Under GDPR, IAM solutions must provide clear audit trails that track data access, modifications, and transfers. Organizations must ensure that users accessing personal data have legitimate business justifications and that access logs are regularly reviewed for compliance. GDPR also grants individuals rights over their personal data, requiring IAM systems to support identity verification for data access requests, rectifications, and deletion requests.

HIPAA enforces stringent data protection measures for healthcare organizations handling electronic protected health information (ePHI). IAM solutions must ensure that only authorized healthcare professionals can access patient records and that all access attempts are logged. Multi-factor authentication (MFA) strengthens authentication controls, reducing the risk of unauthorized access to medical data. Healthcare organizations must implement IAM policies that support data masking, encryption, and automated access reviews to comply with HIPAA regulations. IAM logs help detect unauthorized access attempts and support forensic investigations in case of a data breach.

SOX compliance requires organizations to enforce access controls that protect financial records from unauthorized modifications. IAM solutions help meet these requirements by implementing privilege management, access certification workflows, and audit logging. Financial institutions must enforce segregation of duties (SoD) to prevent conflicts of interest and ensure that no single user has excessive control over financial data. IAM systems automate SoD enforcement, reducing the risk of fraudulent activities and ensuring compliance with SOX auditing standards.

NIST guidelines emphasize the importance of data protection in IAM by recommending continuous monitoring, identity verification, and risk-based authentication. Organizations must implement strong authentication mechanisms, such as biometrics and smart card authentication, to prevent unauthorized access to sensitive data. NIST also promotes the adoption of zero trust security models, ensuring that all access requests are verified based on risk levels before granting data access. IAM solutions must support encryption at rest and in transit to protect data from interception and unauthorized exposure.

ISO 27001 requires organizations to establish an Information Security Management System (ISMS) that includes data protection policies integrated with IAM. Organizations must classify data based on sensitivity levels and enforce IAM controls that align with classification policies. Access to high-risk data must be restricted using strict authentication and authorization mechanisms, reducing the likelihood of data leaks. ISO 27001 audits assess IAM compliance by reviewing access logs, data encryption methods, and incident response procedures. Organizations must demonstrate that IAM policies support data minimization and confidentiality principles outlined in the standard.

IAM solutions enhance data privacy by enabling automated identity lifecycle management. When employees change roles or leave an organization, IAM systems must revoke unnecessary access rights immediately to prevent data exposure. Automated deprovisioning ensures that orphaned accounts do not retain access to confidential information. IAM systems also enforce time-limited access policies for temporary users, such as contractors and third-party vendors, ensuring that data access is revoked once their engagement ends. By automating identity governance, organizations reduce the risk of unauthorized data access and improve compliance with privacy regulations.

Encryption and anonymization are critical IAM strategies for data protection. Organizations must enforce encryption policies that secure sensitive data both in storage and during transmission. IAM solutions integrate with encryption key management systems to enforce strong data security policies. Additionally, data anonymization techniques help organizations protect user identities by masking personal information when it is processed or shared. Compliance frameworks require organizations to document their encryption and anonymization methods to ensure that IAM policies align with data protection best practices.

Incident response and IAM integration play a crucial role in data protection and privacy enforcement. Organizations must establish incident response plans that define how IAM systems detect, report, and mitigate data breaches. IAM solutions support security monitoring by generating alerts for unusual access attempts, privilege escalations, and failed authentication attempts. Security Information and Event Management (SIEM) tools analyze IAM logs to detect anomalies and enforce immediate access restrictions during a security incident. IAM solutions must support forensic investigations by maintaining audit logs that provide detailed records of access events and user activities.

Third-party access management is another critical data protection consideration in IAM. Organizations must enforce strict access controls for external vendors, contractors, and service providers accessing sensitive data. Compliance frameworks require organizations to track and monitor third-party authentication, ensuring that external users do not retain excessive privileges. IAM solutions support third-party identity governance by enforcing just-in-time (JIT) access provisioning, ensuring that vendors only access data for the duration of their engagement. By monitoring third-party access, organizations minimize supply chain security risks and strengthen data protection measures.

IAM dashboards and compliance reporting provide organizations with real-time visibility into data protection enforcement. Security teams use IAM dashboards to monitor data access trends, detect policy violations, and enforce corrective actions. Compliance reports summarize identity governance metrics, access certification findings, and security incident responses. By leveraging IAM analytics, organizations can assess data protection effectiveness and ensure that access policies align with regulatory requirements. Automating compliance reporting reduces manual audit efforts and enhances IAM transparency.

User awareness and training programs support IAM-driven data protection by ensuring that employees understand privacy policies and security best practices. Organizations must educate employees on data classification, access management, and secure authentication practices. IAM solutions reinforce security training by prompting users to acknowledge privacy policies, enforcing password hygiene, and requiring periodic compliance assessments. Strengthening user awareness enhances IAM effectiveness and reduces the risk of human errors that could lead to data breaches.

Data protection and privacy considerations in IAM ensure that sensitive information remains secure, access controls are enforced, and regulatory requirements are met. By integrating IAM with encryption, authentication, monitoring, and compliance reporting, organizations can safeguard personal data, financial records, and healthcare information. Strong IAM policies reduce the risk of unauthorized access, support identity governance, and provide organizations with the tools necessary to maintain compliance with industry standards and legal frameworks.

IAM Compliance for Cloud-Based Environments

Identity and Access Management (IAM) compliance in cloud-based environments is a critical challenge for organizations that store and process sensitive data in the cloud. Unlike traditional on-premises IAM systems, cloud environments require dynamic access controls, continuous monitoring, and compliance enforcement across multiple cloud service providers. Regulatory frameworks such as GDPR, HIPAA, SOX, NIST, and ISO 27001 mandate that organizations implement strict IAM policies to protect cloud resources, ensure data privacy, and prevent unauthorized access. By aligning IAM strategies with compliance requirements, organizations can secure cloud-based identities, enforce least privilege access, and maintain auditability in cloud infrastructures.

Cloud environments introduce new identity management complexities due to the distributed nature of cloud computing, multi-tenancy, and integration with third-party services. Organizations must establish clear IAM policies that define how identities are created, authenticated, and authorized across cloud platforms such as Amazon Web Services (AWS), Microsoft Azure, and Google Cloud Platform (GCP). Role-based access control (RBAC) and attribute-based access control (ABAC) play a key role in ensuring that cloud users have the appropriate level of access based on job responsibilities, contextual attributes, and compliance mandates. Cloud IAM solutions must integrate with on-premises directories and identity providers to maintain consistency in access control enforcement across hybrid environments.

Regulatory compliance requires organizations to implement strong authentication mechanisms to protect cloud-based identities. Multi-factor authentication (MFA) is a mandatory requirement in frameworks such as NIST and ISO 27001, ensuring that users must verify their identity using multiple authentication factors before accessing cloud applications and services. Cloud service providers offer native MFA capabilities, but organizations must enforce MFA policies consistently across all cloud platforms. Adaptive authentication further enhances security by dynamically adjusting authentication requirements based on risk factors such as user location, device trustworthiness, and login behavior. Enforcing MFA across cloud-based environments reduces the risk of credential theft, account takeovers, and unauthorized access to sensitive data.

The shared responsibility model in cloud security requires organizations to manage IAM configurations, access controls, and compliance reporting for cloud resources. While cloud providers secure the underlying infrastructure, organizations are responsible for defining IAM policies, provisioning user roles, and enforcing least privilege access. Compliance regulations mandate that organizations monitor IAM configurations continuously, ensuring that access permissions remain aligned with security policies. Misconfigured IAM settings, such as excessive user privileges, public access to storage buckets, or weak authentication policies, can lead to compliance violations and security breaches. Cloud security posture management (CSPM) solutions help organizations detect IAM misconfigurations, enforce compliance policies, and automate remediation workflows.

Access reviews and certification processes are essential for ensuring IAM compliance in cloud-based environments. Organizations must conduct periodic access reviews to validate that cloud users, service accounts, and privileged identities retain only necessary permissions. Compliance frameworks such as SOX and GDPR require organizations to document access review findings, track privilege escalations, and revoke excessive permissions promptly. Cloud-native IAM tools provide access review dashboards that help security teams visualize user entitlements, detect anomalies, and enforce compliance mandates. Automating access certification processes reduces administrative overhead while ensuring that cloud IAM policies remain aligned with regulatory requirements.

Privileged access management (PAM) in cloud environments ensures that administrative accounts and high-risk identities are properly controlled and monitored. Cloud administrators have elevated permissions that, if misused, can lead to data breaches, compliance violations, and security incidents. IAM solutions must enforce just-in-time (JIT) access provisioning for privileged accounts, granting temporary elevated permissions only when necessary and automatically revoking them after the task is completed. Privileged session recording, audit logging, and anomaly detection help organizations monitor administrative activities in real time, ensuring that compliance mandates for privileged access are met. Organizations must integrate PAM solutions with cloud-native IAM frameworks to maintain full visibility into privileged access activities.

Data protection and privacy regulations require organizations to implement IAM policies that safeguard personal data stored in cloud environments. GDPR mandates that organizations enforce access restrictions on cloud-based personal data, ensuring that only authorized users can process, modify, or transfer personally identifiable information (PII). Cloud IAM solutions must support encryption at rest and in transit, ensuring that sensitive data remains protected from unauthorized access. Compliance reports must document IAM policy enforcement, detailing how user identities are managed, access rights are assigned, and security controls are applied to cloud-based resources. Organizations must implement data masking and anonymization techniques to further protect sensitive data in cloud applications, reducing the risk of compliance violations.

IAM logging and monitoring provide organizations with continuous visibility into access activities within cloud environments. Compliance frameworks such as NIST and ISO 27001 require organizations to maintain detailed audit logs that capture authentication attempts, privilege escalations, and access denials. Cloud service providers offer native logging solutions, such as AWS CloudTrail, Azure Monitor, and Google Cloud Logging, that record IAM events and support forensic investigations. Organizations must aggregate cloud IAM logs in a centralized security information and event management (SIEM) system to detect anomalies, enforce compliance policies, and generate real-time alerts for suspicious access attempts. Automated compliance reporting ensures that organizations can provide auditors with clear evidence of IAM policy enforcement and security monitoring.

Third-party access governance is a critical aspect of IAM compliance in cloud-based environments. Organizations often grant external vendors, contractors, and partners access to cloud resources, increasing the risk of supply chain attacks and data exposure. Compliance frameworks require organizations to monitor and review third-party access privileges, ensuring that external users follow strict authentication and authorization policies. Cloud IAM solutions enable organizations to enforce temporary access policies, requiring third-party users to authenticate using MFA and restricting access to predefined security zones. Continuous monitoring of third-party access activities helps organizations mitigate compliance risks and prevent unauthorized access to cloud data.

Automating IAM compliance in cloud environments reduces complexity, improves efficiency, and ensures continuous enforcement of security policies. Organizations can implement IAM automation tools that integrate with cloud-native IAM frameworks, streamlining identity provisioning, access reviews, and privilege management. Automated policy enforcement ensures that IAM configurations align with compliance requirements, reducing the likelihood of misconfigurations and access control violations. Cloud identity governance solutions help organizations enforce IAM policies across multiple cloud platforms, providing real-time visibility into identity security risks and compliance status. By leveraging IAM automation, organizations improve regulatory adherence while reducing the administrative burden associated with manual compliance enforcement.

IAM compliance training and awareness programs ensure that cloud users understand access control policies, authentication requirements, and compliance obligations. Organizations must educate employees, administrators, and third-party users on best practices for secure access to cloud-based environments. IAM solutions can reinforce security awareness by enforcing policy acknowledgments, displaying compliance reminders, and requiring periodic security training. Strengthening user awareness reduces the risk of human errors that could lead to IAM policy violations and security incidents in cloud infrastructures.

IAM compliance in cloud-based environments requires organizations to enforce access controls, monitor identity activities, and integrate security automation with compliance frameworks. By implementing multi-factor authentication, privileged access management, access reviews, and continuous monitoring, organizations can protect cloud identities and meet regulatory requirements. IAM policies must align with data protection mandates, ensuring that personal data, financial records, and healthcare information remain secure in cloud infrastructures. Automating IAM compliance processes enhances security governance, reduces risk exposure, and ensures that organizations maintain audit readiness across cloud environments.

Managing Privileged Access in Regulatory Frameworks

Privileged access management (PAM) is a critical component of Identity and Access Management (IAM) that ensures the security of high-risk accounts with elevated permissions. Regulatory frameworks such as SOX, GDPR, HIPAA, NIST, and ISO 27001 require organizations to implement strict controls over privileged accounts to prevent unauthorized access, mitigate insider threats, and protect sensitive data. Privileged accounts, including system administrators, database managers, and security personnel, have extensive access to critical systems, making them prime targets for cyberattacks. Managing privileged access within regulatory frameworks involves enforcing least privilege, implementing just-in-time access provisioning, continuously monitoring privileged activities, and ensuring that all actions are auditable.

The Sarbanes-Oxley Act (SOX) enforces strict access control requirements to protect financial data from unauthorized modifications. Organizations must ensure that privileged accounts used for financial reporting systems follow least privilege principles, granting administrative permissions only when necessary. SOX compliance mandates that privileged access be continuously monitored, with all administrative actions logged and reviewed. Organizations must implement multi-factor authentication (MFA) for privileged users, ensuring that unauthorized individuals cannot escalate their privileges. Privileged session management tools help enforce SOX compliance by recording administrator activities, detecting suspicious behavior, and preventing unauthorized changes to financial records.

The General Data Protection Regulation (GDPR) requires organizations to protect personal data by enforcing strict access controls for privileged accounts. Privileged access to personal data must be granted based on business necessity, ensuring that administrators cannot access customer records without justification.

GDPR mandates that organizations implement robust access auditing mechanisms, logging every privileged action performed on systems storing personal data. If a data breach occurs, GDPR requires organizations to investigate privileged access logs to determine whether an unauthorized privileged action contributed to the incident. Implementing role-based access control (RBAC) and attribute-based access control (ABAC) ensures that privileged accounts have only the permissions required for their specific responsibilities, minimizing the risk of data exposure.

The Health Insurance Portability and Accountability Act (HIPAA) enforces strict access controls for protecting electronic protected health information (ePHI). Healthcare organizations must ensure that privileged accounts used by system administrators, medical professionals, and database managers have restricted access to patient records. HIPAA compliance requires organizations to enforce access controls that limit privileged access to authorized users based on job roles and responsibilities. Organizations must log all privileged actions performed on ePHI systems, ensuring that access to patient records is monitored and that unauthorized privilege escalations are detected. Implementing PAM solutions in healthcare environments reduces the risk of insider threats and ensures that privileged users comply with HIPAA security standards.

NIST guidelines provide comprehensive recommendations for managing privileged access within cybersecurity frameworks. Organizations following NIST standards must implement privileged access controls that enforce just-in-time (JIT) privilege escalation, ensuring that administrative permissions are granted temporarily and revoked once tasks are completed. NIST encourages organizations to integrate PAM with zero trust security models, requiring continuous authentication and authorization for privileged actions. Privileged accounts must be continuously monitored for anomalies, with real-time alerts triggered for unusual activities such as unauthorized privilege escalations, multiple failed authentication attempts, or access from unknown devices. By implementing NIST-compliant PAM strategies, organizations strengthen privileged access security and reduce the risk of unauthorized access to sensitive data.

ISO 27001 requires organizations to enforce strict privileged access management policies as part of an Information Security Management System (ISMS). ISO 27001 compliance mandates that organizations define privileged access roles, enforce MFA for privileged users, and implement logging mechanisms that track all privileged actions. Organizations must conduct periodic privileged access reviews, ensuring that privileged accounts remain necessary and that excessive permissions are revoked. Implementing PAM solutions aligned with ISO 27001 enhances access governance by providing detailed audit trails, enforcing session recording, and restricting privileged access to authorized personnel. Regular audits ensure that privileged access policies remain effective and that organizations maintain compliance with ISO 27001 security standards.

Privileged session monitoring is a key requirement for regulatory compliance, ensuring that all privileged user activities are recorded and auditable. Organizations must implement privileged session management tools that track administrative actions, record keystrokes, and capture session activity for forensic investigations. Compliance frameworks require organizations to retain privileged session logs for a specified period, ensuring that security incidents involving privileged accounts can be investigated. Security Information and Event Management (SIEM) systems help organizations analyze privileged session data, detecting security threats and enforcing compliance policies. By implementing privileged session monitoring, organizations gain visibility into administrative activities and ensure that privileged accounts are not misused.

Automating privileged access controls improves compliance by reducing human error and ensuring consistent enforcement of security policies. Organizations must implement automated approval workflows for privileged access requests, requiring multi-level authorization before granting administrative privileges. Automated access certification ensures that privileged accounts are regularly reviewed, with unnecessary permissions revoked based on business requirements. PAM solutions integrate with IAM frameworks to enforce policy-based access controls, ensuring that privileged accounts comply with regulatory requirements. Automation reduces the risk of privilege creep, where users accumulate excessive permissions over time, leading to compliance violations and security risks.

Third-party privileged access management is a critical aspect of regulatory compliance, as organizations frequently grant external vendors, contractors, and service providers temporary access to critical systems. Compliance frameworks require organizations to enforce strict privileged access policies for third-party users, ensuring that access is granted only for specific tasks and is revoked immediately upon completion. Implementing just-in-time access provisioning for third-party users reduces the risk of unauthorized privilege escalations. PAM solutions provide session recording and monitoring for third-party privileged access, ensuring that all administrative actions performed by external users are logged and auditable. Continuous monitoring of third-party privileged access reduces security risks and ensures compliance with regulatory frameworks.

Incident response and privileged access management integration enhance security by enabling organizations to detect and respond to privileged access threats in real time. Compliance frameworks require organizations to establish incident response plans that address privileged account security incidents, including unauthorized privilege escalations, credential misuse, and privilege abuse. IAM solutions integrate with incident response platforms to trigger automated remediation actions, such as revoking privileged access, locking compromised accounts, and enforcing additional authentication requirements. Conducting regular privileged access audits helps organizations identify security gaps, ensuring that PAM policies remain aligned with regulatory compliance requirements.

Privileged access governance training and awareness programs ensure that administrators and security teams understand compliance requirements and security best practices. Organizations must educate privileged users on the risks associated with excessive permissions, the importance of access control policies, and the regulatory consequences of privileged access misuse. IAM solutions reinforce training initiatives by enforcing policy acknowledgments, requiring periodic compliance assessments, and implementing privileged user security awareness programs. Strengthening privileged access governance through education reduces security risks and ensures that privileged users follow compliance policies effectively.

Managing privileged access in regulatory frameworks requires organizations to implement strict access controls, enforce continuous monitoring, and automate compliance enforcement. By aligning PAM strategies with compliance mandates from SOX, GDPR, HIPAA, NIST, and ISO 27001, organizations can protect sensitive data, mitigate insider threats, and maintain audit readiness. Implementing just-in-time privileged access, enforcing multi-factor authentication, and monitoring privileged sessions ensure that administrative accounts are securely managed. Automating privileged access controls and integrating PAM with incident response platforms enhances security resilience, reduces compliance risks, and strengthens IAM governance.

Compliance Challenges in Multi-Cloud and Hybrid Environments

As organizations adopt multi-cloud and hybrid environments to optimize performance, scalability, and cost, ensuring compliance across these diverse infrastructures becomes a significant challenge. Regulatory frameworks such as GDPR, HIPAA, SOX, NIST, and ISO 27001 impose strict access control, data protection, and auditing requirements that organizations must enforce consistently across on-premises systems, private clouds, and public cloud providers like AWS, Microsoft Azure, and Google Cloud Platform. The complexity of managing IAM in such environments increases the risk of misconfigurations, inconsistent security policies, and compliance gaps, making it essential for organizations to implement robust compliance strategies.

A primary compliance challenge in multi-cloud and hybrid environments is the lack of centralized identity and access management. Different cloud providers offer their own IAM solutions, making it difficult for organizations to enforce uniform access policies across multiple platforms. For example, AWS Identity and Access Management (IAM) differs from Azure Active Directory (Azure AD) and Google Cloud IAM in terms of roles, policies, and permission structures. Ensuring compliance with regulations that require strict access control, such as HIPAA's requirement to limit access to electronic protected health information (ePHI), becomes complex when organizations must manage separate IAM configurations for each cloud environment. Implementing federated identity solutions and single sign-on (SSO) helps unify access management across multi-cloud ecosystems, reducing compliance risks.

Data protection and privacy regulations present another compliance challenge in multi-cloud and hybrid environments. Regulations such as GDPR mandate that organizations maintain strict controls over personally identifiable information (PII) and ensure that data processing complies with regional privacy laws. Cloud service providers may store data in different geographic locations, raising concerns about data sovereignty and compliance with data residency laws. Organizations must implement IAM policies that restrict data access based on location, enforce encryption for data in transit and at rest, and maintain audit trails to track data access across cloud environments. Failure to comply with GDPR's data protection requirements can result in significant fines and legal consequences.

Managing privileged access across multi-cloud and hybrid environments is critical for regulatory compliance. Privileged accounts, such as cloud administrators and security engineers, have elevated permissions that, if misused, can lead to data breaches and compliance violations. Compliance frameworks such as SOX require organizations to enforce strict controls over privileged access, ensuring that financial data is protected from unauthorized modifications. However, different cloud platforms have varying privileged access management (PAM) capabilities, making it challenging to enforce consistent security measures. Organizations must implement centralized PAM solutions that provide visibility into privileged accounts across multiple cloud providers, enforce just-in-time (JIT) access provisioning, and monitor privileged activities for compliance violations.

Auditing and monitoring compliance across multi-cloud and hybrid environments require organizations to maintain comprehensive logging and reporting capabilities. Regulatory frameworks mandate that organizations track access attempts, authentication failures, and administrative actions to detect security incidents and ensure compliance with access control policies. However, cloud providers generate separate logs, making it difficult to aggregate and correlate security events. For example, AWS CloudTrail, Azure Monitor, and Google Cloud Logging each provide logs for their respective environments, requiring organizations to implement centralized Security Information and Event Management (SIEM) solutions to analyze IAM events across all platforms. SIEM integration helps organizations detect anomalies, enforce security policies, and generate compliance reports required for regulatory audits.

Multi-cloud and hybrid environments also introduce the challenge of managing third-party access, as organizations frequently grant vendors, contractors, and business partners access to cloud resources. Compliance frameworks require organizations to enforce strict authentication and authorization policies for third-party users, ensuring that external access remains limited to necessary functions. Implementing least privilege access, multi-factor authentication (MFA), and automated access reviews helps organizations mitigate third-party security risks and maintain compliance with regulatory requirements. Continuous monitoring of third-party access logs ensures that external users do not retain excessive privileges after project completion, reducing the risk of supply chain attacks and compliance violations.

IAM misconfigurations are a leading cause of compliance failures in multi-cloud and hybrid environments. Cloud platforms provide flexible identity and access policies, but organizations often struggle to enforce security best practices consistently. For example, improperly configured IAM roles in AWS may grant excessive permissions to users, violating ISO 27001's least privilege requirements. Similarly, unintentional public exposure of cloud storage resources can lead to GDPR compliance violations by exposing personal data. Cloud security posture management (CSPM) tools help organizations identify and remediate IAM misconfigurations, ensuring that access control policies align with compliance mandates and industry best practices.

The complexity of access certification and user lifecycle management in multi-cloud environments increases compliance risks. Organizations must ensure that user access rights are regularly reviewed and updated to align with changing job roles and responsibilities. Compliance frameworks such as NIST and ISO 27001 require organizations to conduct periodic access reviews and revoke unnecessary privileges. However, managing user certifications across multiple cloud platforms manually can be inefficient and error-prone. IAM automation tools streamline access certification processes by generating reports on user entitlements, identifying inactive accounts, and enforcing timely access revocation. Automating user lifecycle management reduces the risk of privilege creep, ensuring continuous compliance with access control policies.

Regulatory compliance also requires organizations to implement zero trust security models in multi-cloud and hybrid environments. Zero trust principles mandate continuous authentication and authorization for all access requests, regardless of network location. Compliance frameworks emphasize the need for risk-based authentication, ensuring that users must verify their identity through adaptive security measures before accessing cloud resources. Implementing zero trust IAM strategies across multi-cloud infrastructures enhances compliance by enforcing strict access controls, monitoring user behavior, and reducing attack surfaces. Organizations must ensure that IAM policies integrate with zero trust architectures to maintain regulatory adherence and protect sensitive data from unauthorized access.

IAM compliance training and awareness programs help mitigate compliance challenges in multi-cloud and hybrid environments. Organizations must educate security teams, administrators, and end-users on regulatory requirements, IAM best practices, and cloud security risks. Compliance frameworks require organizations to conduct security training sessions, reinforcing IAM policies and ensuring that users follow access control guidelines. IAM solutions support compliance training by enforcing policy acknowledgments, displaying compliance dashboards, and requiring periodic security awareness assessments. Strengthening IAM compliance awareness reduces human errors that can lead to security breaches and regulatory violations.

IAM compliance in multi-cloud and hybrid environments requires organizations to implement centralized identity governance, enforce strict access controls, and maintain continuous monitoring of security policies. By integrating federated identity management, privileged access monitoring, SIEM solutions, and automation tools, organizations can mitigate compliance risks and ensure regulatory adherence. Addressing the complexities of multi-cloud IAM through zero trust principles, third-party access management, and proactive misconfiguration detection strengthens security posture and enhances compliance readiness. Organizations must continuously evaluate and adapt IAM strategies to align with evolving regulatory frameworks, ensuring that access control policies remain effective across diverse cloud environments.

Identity Lifecycle Management and Regulatory Adherence

Identity Lifecycle Management (ILM) is a critical aspect of Identity and Access Management (IAM) that ensures users are granted, modified, and revoked access rights based on their role, responsibilities, and employment status. Organizations must align ILM with regulatory frameworks such as GDPR, HIPAA, SOX, NIST, and ISO 27001 to enforce security controls, protect sensitive data, and maintain compliance with legal and industry requirements. Effective ILM processes reduce security risks, prevent unauthorized access, and streamline identity governance, ensuring that users retain only the necessary permissions throughout their tenure.

ILM consists of key stages, including identity provisioning, modification, deprovisioning, and certification. When a new employee, contractor, or third-party vendor joins an organization, their access must be provisioned based on predefined access policies. Role-based access control (RBAC) and attribute-based access control (ABAC) models help assign permissions based on job functions, ensuring that users have the least privilege necessary to perform their duties. Automating identity provisioning reduces the risk of human error, speeds up access approval workflows, and ensures that new users receive appropriate permissions without excessive access rights that could lead to compliance violations.

Regulatory frameworks mandate strict controls over user access provisioning to prevent unauthorized data exposure. GDPR requires organizations to enforce data access restrictions, ensuring that users are granted permissions only when necessary for their job role. Organizations must document access provisioning policies, maintain audit logs, and enforce approval workflows to demonstrate compliance. IAM solutions automate GDPR-compliant provisioning by ensuring that access requests follow strict approval procedures and that personal data access is restricted based on legitimate business purposes. By aligning ILM with GDPR requirements, organizations can ensure that personal data is accessed only by authorized individuals.

HIPAA enforces identity lifecycle controls to protect electronic protected health information (ePHI). Healthcare organizations must ensure that doctors, nurses, and administrative staff receive appropriate access to patient records based on their roles. Identity provisioning must include multi-factor authentication (MFA) and role-based access policies to prevent unauthorized access to medical data. HIPAA compliance audits review ILM policies to verify that healthcare providers enforce strict access controls and regularly update permissions as employee roles change. Automating ILM in healthcare environments reduces the risk of insider threats, improves security, and ensures that only authorized personnel can interact with patient information.

The Sarbanes-Oxley Act (SOX) requires organizations to implement identity lifecycle controls to protect financial records and prevent unauthorized transactions. User provisioning must be governed by strict approval workflows that ensure financial system access is granted only to employees who require it. Organizations must enforce separation of duties (SoD), ensuring that no single user can execute conflicting financial functions that could lead to fraud. ILM processes must include periodic reviews of financial system access to detect privilege accumulation and revoke excessive permissions. IAM automation enhances SOX compliance by enforcing strict identity provisioning policies and maintaining detailed logs of access assignments.

User identity modification is a crucial component of ILM that ensures permissions are adjusted when an employee changes roles, departments, or responsibilities. Regulatory frameworks require organizations to conduct regular access reviews to verify that user permissions remain aligned with job functions. NIST guidelines emphasize the importance of continuous monitoring, recommending that organizations implement automated identity governance tools that detect changes in user roles and adjust access permissions accordingly. Failure to update access rights when employees change positions increases the risk of privilege creep, where users accumulate unnecessary permissions over time, leading to potential security threats and compliance violations.

ISO 27001 mandates that organizations enforce ILM policies that ensure access rights are regularly reviewed and updated. Access modification processes must follow predefined governance policies, ensuring that permissions are adjusted or revoked as soon as an employee's responsibilities change. IAM automation streamlines ISO 27001 compliance by triggering access reviews whenever user roles are modified, ensuring that permissions remain accurate and aligned with security policies. Organizations must maintain access logs that document every change in user permissions, providing auditors with a clear record of ILM enforcement.

User deprovisioning is one of the most critical aspects of ILM for compliance and security. When employees leave an organization, their access rights must be revoked immediately to prevent unauthorized access to corporate systems. Regulatory frameworks require organizations to establish structured offboarding processes that remove access to applications, databases, and cloud environments upon employee termination. IAM automation ensures that deprovisioning occurs in real time, preventing orphaned accounts that could be exploited by attackers or disgruntled employees. Implementing automated deprovisioning policies ensures that access termination is enforced consistently across all systems, reducing security risks and ensuring compliance.

ILM compliance also requires organizations to manage third-party identities effectively. Vendors, contractors, and external business partners often require temporary access to corporate resources, increasing the risk of data exposure and compliance violations. IAM solutions enforce just-in-time (JIT) access provisioning for third-party users, granting access only for the duration of their engagement. Organizations must track and monitor third-party access, ensuring that external users do not retain unnecessary privileges after project completion. Regulatory frameworks require organizations to conduct periodic reviews of third-party access, ensuring that permissions are revoked when no longer needed. IAM governance solutions automate third-party identity management, reducing security risks and maintaining compliance with industry regulations.

Access certification processes ensure that ILM policies remain effective and compliant with regulatory requirements. Organizations must conduct periodic access reviews to verify that user permissions are still necessary and aligned with job functions. Compliance frameworks such as SOX and GDPR require organizations to maintain detailed certification reports, documenting access reviews and privilege adjustments. IAM automation simplifies access certification by generating compliance reports, identifying access anomalies, and enforcing access revocation when necessary. Automating certification workflows reduces administrative overhead, improves audit readiness, and ensures that ILM policies remain aligned with regulatory mandates.

IAM analytics and reporting enhance ILM compliance by providing visibility into user access trends, privilege modifications, and deprovisioning activities. Organizations must generate compliance reports that document ILM enforcement, ensuring that auditors can verify access governance policies. IAM dashboards provide real-time insights into identity lifecycle activities, enabling security teams to detect unauthorized access attempts, privilege escalations, and orphaned accounts. Automated compliance reporting helps organizations track ILM effectiveness, ensuring that access control policies remain enforced and that regulatory requirements are met.

Employee training and awareness programs support ILM compliance by ensuring that users understand identity governance policies and security best practices. Organizations must educate employees on access request procedures, privilege management, and data protection responsibilities. IAM solutions reinforce training initiatives by enforcing policy acknowledgments, requiring periodic compliance assessments, and providing users with real-time security alerts. Strengthening ILM awareness reduces human errors that could lead to compliance violations and unauthorized data access.

Identity Lifecycle Management is a fundamental component of IAM compliance, ensuring that user access rights are provisioned, modified, and revoked in accordance with regulatory requirements. By automating ILM processes, enforcing access certification, and integrating identity governance tools, organizations can reduce security risks, prevent privilege accumulation, and maintain compliance with frameworks such as GDPR, HIPAA, SOX, NIST, and ISO 27001. Strong ILM policies enhance access control, improve audit readiness, and ensure that identity governance remains aligned with regulatory standards.

Just-in-Time (JIT) Access and Compliance Controls

Just-in-Time (JIT) access is an advanced Identity and Access Management (IAM) strategy that grants temporary access privileges to users only when needed and for a limited duration. This approach aligns with compliance frameworks such as SOX, GDPR, HIPAA, NIST, and ISO 27001, which mandate strict access control measures to prevent unauthorized access, enforce least privilege, and reduce security risks. JIT access enhances security by ensuring that users do not retain unnecessary or excessive privileges, minimizing the risk of insider threats, credential abuse, and privilege escalation attacks. Organizations implementing JIT access controls can improve regulatory adherence while strengthening overall security posture.

Regulatory frameworks emphasize the importance of least privilege access, requiring organizations to ensure that users receive only the permissions necessary for their job functions. Traditional access models often grant persistent permissions, leading to privilege accumulation and increased attack surfaces. JIT access eliminates this risk by granting temporary access only when explicitly requested and approved. In compliance with SOX, organizations must restrict access to financial systems and data, ensuring that only authorized personnel can modify financial records. JIT access ensures that privileged users, such as auditors or financial analysts, receive temporary access to sensitive financial data only when required, reducing the risk of fraudulent activity or unauthorized modifications.

GDPR mandates strict data access controls to protect personal information from unauthorized access and processing. Organizations must ensure that user access to customer data is limited and justified based on business needs. JIT access supports GDPR compliance by preventing employees from retaining continuous access to personal data, instead requiring explicit access requests for each data interaction. This approach enforces data minimization principles by ensuring that users access personal data only for specific tasks and for a predefined duration. By integrating JIT access with authentication and approval workflows, organizations can document and audit every access request, providing evidence of compliance with GDPR requirements.

HIPAA compliance requires healthcare organizations to protect electronic protected health information (ePHI) by implementing strict access controls and auditing mechanisms. JIT access helps enforce HIPAA security standards by ensuring that medical staff, administrative personnel, and third-party service providers receive access to ePHI only when necessary. For example, a specialist consulting on a patient's case can request temporary access to medical records, which is automatically revoked after the consultation. Implementing JIT access in healthcare environments reduces the risk of unauthorized ePHI exposure, prevents insider threats, and ensures that healthcare providers comply with HIPAA's access control mandates.

NIST guidelines emphasize the importance of risk-based access controls and continuous authentication to mitigate security threats. JIT access aligns with NIST recommendations by enforcing dynamic, time-limited access that adapts based on security risks and business needs. Organizations implementing JIT access under NIST frameworks must integrate approval workflows, risk-based authentication, and real-time monitoring to ensure that temporary access is granted only under predefined conditions. Security Information and Event Management (SIEM) solutions help detect anomalies in JIT access requests, triggering automated responses if suspicious activity is detected. By enforcing JIT access policies, organizations reduce their exposure to insider threats and unauthorized access attempts.

ISO 27001 requires organizations to implement access control mechanisms that align with the principle of least privilege and risk mitigation strategies. JIT access supports ISO 27001 compliance by ensuring that users do not maintain unnecessary access to critical systems, reducing the attack surface and improving security governance. Organizations must establish JIT access policies that define approval requirements, authentication steps, and expiration conditions for temporary privileges. IAM solutions automate JIT access provisioning, ensuring that access requests follow security policies and compliance standards. By integrating JIT access with audit logging and reporting tools, organizations can provide regulators with clear evidence of compliance during ISO 27001 audits.

Privileged Access Management (PAM) plays a crucial role in JIT access implementation, ensuring that administrative accounts and high-risk identities receive access only when necessary. Traditional privileged access models often grant persistent administrative privileges, increasing the risk of credential misuse and insider threats. JIT access enhances PAM security by enforcing temporary privilege escalation, granting administrative rights only for specific tasks and automatically revoking them afterward. Compliance frameworks such as SOX and HIPAA require organizations to monitor privileged access activities and ensure that administrative actions are justified and auditable. By integrating JIT access with PAM solutions, organizations can enforce real-time privileged session monitoring, record administrative activities, and reduce compliance risks.

JIT access also enhances security in multi-cloud and hybrid environments, where organizations must manage access across multiple cloud platforms and on-premises systems. Compliance regulations require organizations to enforce consistent access control policies across all environments, preventing excessive permissions and unauthorized access. Cloud service providers offer JIT access features that allow organizations to provision time-limited access to cloud resources, reducing the risk of persistent privileges. By implementing JIT access policies across cloud IAM frameworks such as AWS IAM, Azure AD, and Google Cloud IAM, organizations can maintain compliance with security and data protection regulations.

Organizations implementing JIT access must establish approval workflows that ensure temporary access requests are validated before being granted. Compliance frameworks require organizations to document access approvals, ensuring that security teams can review and audit all JIT access activities. Automated approval workflows streamline this process by integrating with IAM platforms, requiring managers or security officers to approve high-risk access requests before granting temporary permissions. Implementing multi-factor authentication (MFA) for JIT access approvals adds an additional layer of security, ensuring that only verified users receive access to sensitive systems and data.

JIT access monitoring and auditing are essential for maintaining compliance with regulatory frameworks. Organizations must track all temporary access requests, approvals, and revocations to ensure that security policies are enforced consistently. Compliance regulations require organizations to generate audit logs that document JIT access activities, allowing security teams to review user interactions and detect potential security incidents. IAM solutions provide real-time dashboards and automated reporting tools that help organizations analyze JIT access patterns, detect anomalies, and enforce corrective actions. Continuous monitoring ensures that JIT access policies remain effective and that compliance obligations are met.

Third-party access management is another critical area where JIT access enhances compliance. Organizations frequently grant external vendors, contractors, and service providers temporary access to internal systems, increasing the risk of data breaches and compliance violations. JIT access ensures that third-party users receive access only when necessary and for a predefined duration, preventing them from retaining persistent permissions. Compliance frameworks require organizations to track and monitor third-party access activities, ensuring that external users follow strict authentication and authorization policies. By integrating JIT access with third-party identity governance solutions, organizations can enforce security controls and mitigate third-party security risks.

Employee training and awareness programs support JIT access adoption by ensuring that users understand compliance requirements and security best practices. Organizations must educate employees on the benefits of JIT access, access request procedures, and regulatory requirements related to temporary privileges. IAM solutions enforce security training by prompting users to acknowledge JIT access policies, requiring periodic compliance assessments, and providing real-time security alerts. Strengthening security awareness helps organizations prevent unauthorized access, reduce human errors, and ensure that JIT access policies remain aligned with regulatory standards.

Just-in-Time (JIT) access is a powerful compliance control that ensures users receive only the necessary privileges for a limited period, reducing security risks and aligning with regulatory frameworks. By integrating JIT access with IAM, PAM, and monitoring solutions, organizations can enforce least privilege access, prevent unauthorized privilege escalation, and maintain auditability. Implementing automated approval workflows, continuous monitoring, and third-party access controls enhances security governance and ensures compliance with industry regulations.

Zero Trust Architecture and Its Role in Compliance

Zero Trust Architecture (ZTA) is a modern cybersecurity framework that enforces strict identity verification and continuous monitoring before granting access to systems, applications, and data. Unlike traditional security models that assume trust within corporate networks, Zero Trust operates on the principle that no user, device, or network component should be inherently trusted. Regulatory frameworks such as SOX, GDPR, HIPAA, NIST, and ISO 27001 emphasize strict access controls, continuous authentication, and real-time monitoring, making Zero Trust a critical approach for ensuring compliance. By implementing ZTA, organizations can enforce least privilege access, reduce attack surfaces, and enhance regulatory adherence.

Regulatory requirements mandate that organizations enforce robust authentication and authorization controls to prevent unauthorized access. The Zero Trust model aligns with these requirements by enforcing identity-based access decisions that verify user credentials, device posture, and contextual risk factors before granting access. Under SOX, organizations must protect financial data by ensuring that only authorized personnel can modify or view financial records. Traditional perimeter-based security models fail to meet SOX compliance requirements due to evolving threats such as credential theft and insider attacks. Zero Trust ensures compliance by implementing multi-factor authentication (MFA), role-based access control (RBAC), and real-time access monitoring to protect financial systems.

GDPR mandates strict data protection measures to prevent unauthorized access and data breaches involving personally identifiable information (PII). Organizations processing personal data must implement security controls that minimize unauthorized exposure and demonstrate compliance with data protection principles. Zero Trust enhances GDPR compliance by enforcing dynamic access policies that evaluate user behavior, device health, and contextual risk before granting access to customer data. Adaptive authentication and continuous access validation ensure that only legitimate users can access PII, reducing the risk of unauthorized data processing. Organizations must also maintain audit logs that document all access attempts and security events, providing regulators with proof of GDPR adherence.

HIPAA enforces stringent security controls to protect electronic protected health information (ePHI). Healthcare organizations must ensure that only authorized personnel can access patient records, medical applications, and billing systems. Zero Trust enhances HIPAA compliance by implementing continuous authentication, risk-based access controls, and micro-segmentation to restrict data access. Traditional security models that rely on network-based trust expose ePHI to risks such as credential misuse and lateral movement attacks. By implementing Zero Trust, healthcare providers can enforce granular access policies that verify user identity, location, and device security posture before allowing access to medical records. Continuous monitoring ensures that unauthorized access attempts trigger alerts, preventing security incidents and regulatory violations.

NIST promotes Zero Trust as a foundational cybersecurity strategy to strengthen access controls and mitigate security risks. The NIST 800-207 framework outlines best practices for implementing Zero Trust, including continuous authentication, least privilege enforcement, and data segmentation. Organizations adopting Zero Trust under NIST guidelines must ensure that every access request is verified dynamically, preventing attackers from exploiting static credentials or compromised accounts. Security Information and Event Management (SIEM) solutions integrate with Zero Trust frameworks to detect anomalous behavior, enforce compliance policies, and generate real-time security reports. By aligning Zero Trust with NIST requirements, organizations can enhance cybersecurity resilience while maintaining regulatory compliance.

ISO 27001 requires organizations to implement risk-based security controls that protect sensitive data from unauthorized access. Zero Trust supports ISO 27001 compliance by enforcing identity-based access control, continuous risk assessment, and encryption of sensitive data. Organizations must define and enforce access policies that grant least privilege access to users and devices based on security risk analysis. Zero Trust Identity and Access Management (IAM) solutions enable organizations to monitor user activities, detect policy violations, and generate compliance reports for audit purposes. Implementing Zero Trust principles reduces the risk of unauthorized data access, ensuring alignment with ISO 27001 security controls.

Micro-segmentation is a core component of Zero Trust that restricts user and device access based on defined security policies. Traditional network security models grant broad access to users within internal corporate networks, increasing the risk of lateral movement attacks. Zero Trust enforces micro-segmentation by isolating applications, databases, and cloud workloads, ensuring that users can only access resources explicitly authorized by security policies. Compliance frameworks such as HIPAA and GDPR require organizations to enforce strict access restrictions for sensitive data, making micro-segmentation an essential security measure. Organizations must continuously evaluate and update micro-segmentation policies to adapt to evolving security threats and compliance mandates.

Privileged Access Management (PAM) integrates with Zero Trust to enforce strict controls over administrative accounts and high-risk identities. Compliance frameworks mandate that privileged users receive only the necessary permissions to perform specific tasks, reducing the risk of privilege misuse and insider threats. Traditional privileged access models often grant persistent administrator privileges, increasing the risk of credential abuse. Zero Trust eliminates persistent privileged access by enforcing just-in-time (JIT) access provisioning, granting temporary administrative permissions only when required and automatically revoking them after task completion. Privileged session monitoring and forensic logging provide organizations with visibility into administrative activities, ensuring compliance with SOX, NIST, and ISO 27001 regulations.

Zero Trust strengthens compliance in multi-cloud and hybrid environments by enforcing consistent access policies across cloud platforms, data centers, and remote workforces. Regulatory frameworks require organizations to maintain strict control over cloud-based access, preventing unauthorized exposure of sensitive data. Cloud Identity and Access Management (IAM) solutions integrate with Zero Trust to enforce adaptive authentication, least privilege access, and continuous session monitoring for cloud applications and services. Organizations must implement unified security policies that extend across multi-cloud environments, ensuring compliance with industry standards and regulatory mandates. Zero Trust enhances cloud security by preventing unauthorized access, detecting policy violations, and automating compliance reporting.

Zero Trust also addresses third-party access compliance challenges by enforcing strict authentication and authorization controls for external vendors, contractors, and business partners. Regulatory frameworks require organizations to limit third-party access to sensitive data and enforce strict monitoring policies. Zero Trust enforces just-in-time access for third-party users, granting time-limited permissions that expire automatically after project completion. Organizations must continuously monitor third-party access activities, ensuring that external users comply with security policies and compliance requirements. Zero Trust reduces the risk of third-party security breaches by restricting access to only the necessary resources while preventing unauthorized privilege escalation.

Continuous monitoring and compliance automation are key aspects of Zero Trust implementation. Compliance frameworks require organizations to maintain audit trails that document user access, authentication attempts, and security incidents. Zero Trust integrates with security analytics platforms to provide real-time compliance monitoring, detecting unauthorized access attempts and enforcing policy-based remediation. Automated compliance reporting ensures that organizations can generate regulatory audit reports that demonstrate adherence to access control policies, privilege management requirements, and data protection standards. By leveraging Zero Trust for continuous compliance monitoring, organizations can detect security threats proactively and maintain regulatory adherence.

Security awareness and training programs support Zero Trust adoption by educating employees, administrators, and third-party users on access control policies and compliance requirements. Organizations must implement ongoing training initiatives that reinforce the importance of Zero Trust security principles, including risk-based authentication, least privilege access, and continuous monitoring. IAM solutions integrate security awareness training with Zero Trust frameworks by enforcing policy acknowledgments, requiring periodic compliance assessments, and providing real-time security alerts. Strengthening security awareness ensures that users follow Zero Trust access policies, reducing compliance violations and security risks.

Zero Trust Architecture provides organizations with a comprehensive security framework that enforces compliance with regulatory requirements, prevents unauthorized access, and reduces the attack surface. By implementing identity-based access controls, continuous monitoring, micro-segmentation, and privileged access management, organizations can achieve compliance with SOX, GDPR, HIPAA, NIST, and ISO 27001 while strengthening cybersecurity resilience. Zero Trust transforms access management by eliminating implicit trust, enforcing dynamic authentication policies, and automating compliance monitoring to protect sensitive data and critical systems.

Secure Authentication Methods and Compliance Standards

Secure authentication methods are a fundamental component of Identity and Access Management (IAM), ensuring that only authorized users can access critical systems, applications, and data. Regulatory frameworks such as SOX, GDPR, HIPAA, NIST, and ISO 27001 mandate the use of strong authentication mechanisms to protect sensitive information from unauthorized access and data breaches. Organizations must implement authentication controls that align with these compliance standards, including multi-factor authentication (MFA), passwordless authentication, biometrics, and risk-based authentication. By enforcing secure authentication methods, organizations can reduce the risk of credential-based attacks, enhance identity security, and maintain regulatory compliance.

Multi-factor authentication (MFA) is one of the most widely adopted authentication methods for compliance with security regulations. MFA requires users to verify their identity using at least two different authentication factors: something they know (password or PIN), something they have (security token or smart card), and something they are (biometric data such as fingerprint or facial recognition). Regulatory frameworks mandate MFA as a critical security measure to prevent unauthorized access. Under SOX, organizations must protect financial data by enforcing strong authentication controls for employees accessing financial reporting systems. GDPR requires organizations to implement authentication measures that prevent unauthorized access to personal data, and MFA ensures that only verified users can interact with customer information.

HIPAA enforces authentication requirements for healthcare organizations to safeguard electronic protected health information (ePHI). Hospitals, clinics, and healthcare providers must implement secure authentication mechanisms to ensure that only authorized medical personnel can access patient records and prescribing systems. MFA strengthens HIPAA compliance by requiring doctors, nurses, and administrative staff to verify their identities before accessing sensitive data. Biometric authentication, such as fingerprint scanning or facial recognition, provides an additional layer of security in healthcare environments, ensuring that patient data remains protected from unauthorized access. Implementing strong authentication measures in healthcare organizations reduces the risk of data breaches and ensures compliance with HIPAA security regulations.

The National Institute of Standards and Technology (NIST) provides detailed guidelines on authentication security under its Special Publication 800-63. NIST recommends organizations implement passwordless authentication and adaptive authentication models that evaluate user behavior, device trustworthiness, and contextual risk factors. Traditional password-based authentication is highly vulnerable to attacks such as phishing, credential stuffing, and brute force attempts. To mitigate these risks, NIST recommends organizations enforce authentication methods that minimize reliance on passwords and instead use cryptographic authentication techniques, smart cards, or biometric authentication. By aligning authentication policies with NIST standards, organizations can enhance security while ensuring compliance with federal security regulations.

ISO 27001 requires organizations to implement strong authentication policies as part of their Information Security Management System (ISMS). Secure authentication mechanisms must be enforced to protect sensitive business data, ensuring that unauthorized users cannot access critical assets. Organizations must define authentication policies that specify minimum password complexity requirements, session timeout controls, and access revocation procedures. ISO 27001 audits evaluate authentication practices to ensure compliance with data protection and security requirements. Implementing MFA, passwordless authentication, and continuous authentication monitoring aligns with ISO 27001's emphasis on secure access control.

Passwordless authentication methods provide a more secure alternative to traditional password-based authentication. Regulations encourage organizations to reduce reliance on passwords due to their vulnerability to credential theft and user-generated weaknesses. Passwordless authentication leverages cryptographic keys, smart cards, one-time passcodes (OTP), and biometric verification to authenticate users without requiring a password. Implementing passwordless authentication ensures compliance with security frameworks that emphasize strong authentication controls. Organizations using passwordless authentication eliminate risks associated with weak passwords while improving user experience and security.

Risk-based authentication (RBA) enhances compliance by dynamically adjusting authentication requirements based on real-time risk analysis. RBA evaluates contextual factors such as login location, device reputation, access history, and user behavior to determine authentication requirements. If a login attempt is detected from an unusual location or an unrecognized device, RBA triggers additional authentication steps such as MFA or biometric verification. Compliance frameworks require organizations to enforce security controls that detect and respond to authentication anomalies. By implementing RBA, organizations can strengthen security while ensuring compliance with regulatory requirements that mandate adaptive authentication models.

Federated authentication streamlines secure access across multiple platforms and services while maintaining compliance with access control regulations. Federated identity management allows users to authenticate once and gain access to multiple systems using a single set of credentials. Security Assertion Markup Language (SAML), OpenID Connect (OIDC), and OAuth 2.0 enable secure authentication across cloud applications, reducing password fatigue and improving access governance. Compliance frameworks such as GDPR require organizations to maintain strong authentication policies while ensuring seamless access to cloud-based services. Federated authentication enables secure and compliant access to cloud environments, reducing security risks associated with password reuse.

Single sign-on (SSO) solutions enhance authentication security by allowing users to authenticate once and access multiple applications without re-entering credentials. SSO reduces the risk of password-related security incidents by minimizing the number of passwords users must manage. Compliance frameworks emphasize SSO as a secure authentication method that enhances identity governance while ensuring controlled access to sensitive data. Organizations implementing SSO must enforce strong authentication policies, ensuring that SSO solutions integrate with MFA, risk-based authentication, and session management controls. Secure SSO implementations align with regulatory mandates that require robust access control measures to protect sensitive business data.

Session management and authentication logging are essential components of compliance enforcement. Organizations must implement session timeout policies that automatically terminate inactive sessions to prevent unauthorized access. Compliance frameworks require organizations to maintain audit logs that track authentication attempts, failed login events, and privilege escalations. IAM solutions integrate authentication logging with Security Information and Event Management (SIEM) tools, ensuring that authentication events are continuously monitored for compliance violations. Generating authentication reports allows organizations to demonstrate compliance with regulatory requirements, ensuring that secure authentication practices are enforced consistently.

Third-party authentication security is a critical compliance consideration, as organizations frequently grant external vendors, contractors, and partners access to internal systems. Compliance regulations require organizations to enforce strong authentication policies for third-party users, ensuring that external identities follow the same security standards as internal employees. Organizations must require third-party users to authenticate using MFA, enforce time-restricted access policies, and monitor authentication logs for suspicious activities. By integrating third-party authentication controls with IAM solutions, organizations can mitigate security risks while ensuring compliance with industry standards.

Employee training and awareness programs support authentication compliance by ensuring that users understand secure authentication practices, password hygiene, and MFA requirements. Organizations must educate employees on the risks of phishing attacks, credential theft, and social engineering tactics that compromise authentication security. IAM solutions reinforce authentication training by enforcing periodic security assessments, displaying authentication policy reminders, and requiring users to acknowledge security guidelines. Strengthening authentication awareness reduces human errors that could lead to compliance violations and security breaches.

Secure authentication methods are essential for regulatory compliance, ensuring that access control policies align with SOX, GDPR, HIPAA, NIST, and ISO 27001 security mandates. By implementing MFA, passwordless authentication, risk-based authentication, and federated identity management, organizations can strengthen identity security while maintaining compliance with industry regulations. Secure authentication frameworks enhance user protection, prevent credential-based attacks, and ensure that organizations enforce regulatory authentication controls effectively.

Identity Federation and Regulatory Implications

Identity federation is a framework that enables users to access multiple systems and applications across different organizations or domains using a single set of credentials. This approach enhances security, reduces password fatigue, and improves user experience while ensuring compliance with regulatory requirements such as SOX, GDPR, HIPAA, NIST, and ISO 27001. By centralizing authentication and authorization through identity providers (IdPs), identity federation simplifies access management, enforces strong authentication controls, and ensures that user identities remain secure across interconnected environments.

Regulatory frameworks require organizations to enforce strict identity management policies to prevent unauthorized access, data breaches, and compliance violations. The Sarbanes-Oxley Act (SOX) mandates that organizations implement robust access controls to protect financial systems and ensure that only authorized users can access critical financial data. Identity federation supports SOX compliance by enabling organizations to enforce centralized authentication, role-based access control (RBAC), and real-time identity monitoring. By integrating federated authentication with Security Information and Event Management (SIEM) solutions, organizations can generate compliance reports that track authentication attempts, privilege escalations, and access anomalies.

The General Data Protection Regulation (GDPR) enforces strict data protection measures to safeguard personal data from unauthorized access and processing. Organizations using identity federation must ensure that authentication requests and identity data exchanges comply with GDPR principles, including data minimization, consent management, and encryption. Federated identity solutions must implement privacy-preserving mechanisms that prevent the unnecessary sharing of personally identifiable information (PII) between identity providers and service providers. Organizations must also document identity federation policies, ensuring that user consent is obtained before processing personal data for authentication purposes. Compliance with GDPR requires organizations to enforce security controls that protect federated authentication tokens, ensuring that identity federation does not expose user data to unauthorized parties.

HIPAA enforces strict identity and access management controls to protect electronic protected health information (ePHI). Healthcare organizations using identity federation must ensure that federated authentication mechanisms comply with HIPAA security rules, enforcing multi-factor authentication (MFA), session monitoring, and encryption for authentication data. Federated identity management allows healthcare providers to securely authenticate users across different systems, ensuring that only authorized personnel can access patient records. Organizations must also implement audit logging for federated authentication events, ensuring that access to ePHI remains traceable and auditable. By integrating identity federation with access governance policies, healthcare organizations can enhance security while maintaining HIPAA compliance.

The National Institute of Standards and Technology (NIST) provides guidelines on identity federation under NIST Special Publication 800-63. NIST requires organizations to implement strong authentication and federation protocols that ensure secure identity verification across systems. NIST-compliant identity federation solutions must enforce cryptographic authentication, token-based security, and continuous access validation. Organizations must implement risk-based authentication mechanisms that dynamically adjust authentication requirements based on user behavior, device trust levels, and contextual risks. NIST guidelines emphasize the importance of identity proofing in federated environments, ensuring that users are properly verified before being granted federated authentication privileges. By aligning identity federation policies with NIST standards, organizations can strengthen security while ensuring compliance with federal cybersecurity regulations.

ISO 27001 mandates that organizations enforce strict identity and access management policies to protect sensitive data from unauthorized access. Identity federation supports ISO 27001 compliance by ensuring that authentication and authorization processes are centrally managed, reducing the risk of identity-related security breaches. Organizations implementing identity federation must define security policies that regulate how authentication credentials, identity assertions, and access tokens are exchanged between identity providers and relying parties. ISO 27001 compliance requires organizations to document identity federation configurations, ensuring that authentication requests are logged, monitored, and reviewed for security risks. Implementing federated identity governance enhances compliance by providing real-time visibility into identity authentication events and access control enforcement.

Security Assertion Markup Language (SAML), OpenID Connect (OIDC), and OAuth 2.0 are widely used identity federation protocols that enable secure authentication and authorization across federated domains. These protocols ensure that authentication credentials are not directly shared with service providers, reducing the risk of credential exposure and identity theft. Compliance frameworks require organizations to implement strong token security policies that prevent unauthorized access to authentication tokens and identity assertions. Organizations must enforce token expiration policies, ensuring that authentication tokens do not remain valid beyond necessary time frames. Identity federation solutions must also implement cryptographic signing and encryption for authentication assertions, ensuring that authentication data is protected from interception and tampering.

Multi-cloud and hybrid environments present additional compliance challenges for identity federation, as organizations must enforce consistent authentication policies across different cloud platforms and on-premises systems. Compliance regulations require organizations to maintain strict access control policies that prevent unauthorized access to cloud-based data and applications. Identity federation enables organizations to centralize authentication across cloud providers such as AWS, Microsoft Azure, and Google Cloud, ensuring that users can securely access cloud resources without managing multiple credentials. Organizations must implement cross-cloud identity federation policies that align with compliance requirements, ensuring that authentication events are logged, monitored, and reviewed for security risks.

Privileged access management (PAM) plays a critical role in identity federation compliance, ensuring that privileged users receive federated access only when necessary. Compliance frameworks such as SOX and ISO 27001 require organizations to enforce strict privileged access controls, ensuring that administrative users do not retain persistent access to sensitive systems. Federated identity governance solutions integrate with PAM to enforce just-in-time (JIT) access provisioning, granting temporary privileged access based on predefined security policies. Organizations must implement session monitoring, privileged access logging, and approval workflows for federated privileged access requests, ensuring compliance with regulatory mandates.

Third-party identity federation introduces additional compliance risks, as organizations often extend federated authentication capabilities to external vendors, contractors, and business partners. Regulatory frameworks require organizations to enforce strict identity verification and authentication policies for third-party users, ensuring that external entities do not retain excessive access privileges. Identity federation solutions must implement time-limited access policies for third-party authentication, requiring continuous authorization for extended access. Organizations must also monitor federated authentication logs to detect unauthorized third-party access attempts and enforce remediation actions when security violations occur.

IAM compliance training and awareness programs ensure that employees, administrators, and third-party users understand identity federation policies and security best practices. Organizations must provide security training sessions that educate users on secure authentication, access control enforcement, and regulatory compliance requirements for federated authentication. IAM solutions integrate compliance training with identity federation policies by enforcing policy acknowledgments, requiring periodic security assessments, and displaying real-time security notifications. Strengthening security awareness reduces identity-related security risks and ensures that federated authentication policies align with compliance standards.

Identity federation enhances security and compliance by centralizing authentication, enforcing strong access controls, and reducing credential management risks. By implementing secure identity federation protocols, multi-factor authentication, and continuous monitoring, organizations can comply with regulatory frameworks such as SOX, GDPR, HIPAA, NIST, and ISO 27001 while maintaining secure access governance. Identity federation solutions enable organizations to streamline authentication across multiple domains, enforce least privilege access, and enhance identity security, ensuring that authentication processes align with compliance mandates.

Automating Compliance Controls in IAM

Automating compliance controls in Identity and Access Management (IAM) is essential for organizations to efficiently enforce security policies, minimize human error, and ensure continuous regulatory adherence. Compliance frameworks such as SOX, GDPR, HIPAA, NIST, and ISO 27001 require strict access controls, auditing mechanisms, and security policies to protect sensitive data. Manual compliance enforcement is time-consuming, prone to misconfigurations, and difficult to scale across complex IT environments. By leveraging automation in IAM, organizations can streamline compliance workflows, enforce least privilege access, and maintain real-time monitoring to detect and prevent security violations.

IAM automation enhances compliance by enforcing standardized identity governance policies that regulate how users are provisioned, authenticated, and authorized. Role-based access control (RBAC) and attribute-based access control (ABAC) models are automated to ensure that users receive only the necessary permissions based on job functions and contextual attributes. Automating access control policies aligns with regulatory requirements that mandate strict enforcement of least privilege access. Under SOX, organizations must prevent unauthorized modifications to financial records by ensuring that employees and contractors do not accumulate excessive privileges. IAM automation continuously evaluates user roles, adjusting permissions dynamically to comply with SOX requirements while maintaining operational efficiency.

General Data Protection Regulation (GDPR) mandates that organizations protect personal data by enforcing access restrictions, ensuring that only authorized users can process or view sensitive information. IAM automation helps organizations comply with GDPR by implementing automated access provisioning and deprovisioning workflows that remove unnecessary privileges when an employee's role changes or they leave the organization. Automating identity lifecycle management ensures that access rights are granted and revoked in real time, reducing the risk of orphaned accounts that could lead to data breaches. IAM compliance automation also generates detailed audit logs that document all access requests, approvals, and modifications, providing regulators with clear evidence of GDPR adherence.

The Health Insurance Portability and Accountability Act (HIPAA) requires healthcare organizations to implement security measures that protect electronic protected health information (ePHI). IAM automation enhances HIPAA compliance by enforcing multi-factor authentication (MFA), implementing session monitoring, and ensuring that healthcare providers access patient data only when necessary. Automated privileged access management (PAM) controls restrict administrative privileges, ensuring that medical personnel, IT administrators, and third-party service providers do not retain excessive access to healthcare systems. IAM automation also facilitates continuous monitoring of authentication attempts, detecting anomalies that could indicate security threats, such as unauthorized access attempts or privilege escalations.

NIST guidelines emphasize the importance of continuous compliance monitoring and automated security enforcement to prevent identity-related threats. IAM automation aligns with NIST compliance requirements by enforcing real-time risk-based authentication (RBA), which dynamically adjusts authentication requirements based on user behavior, device trust level, and geographic location. Automated compliance controls continuously evaluate access requests against predefined security policies, preventing unauthorized access attempts from high-risk locations or untrusted devices. Organizations implementing IAM automation under NIST guidelines can integrate machine learning-based anomaly detection to identify suspicious access patterns, ensuring proactive threat mitigation.

ISO 27001 requires organizations to implement an Information Security Management System (ISMS) that enforces access control, identity verification, and security policy adherence. IAM automation supports ISO 27001 compliance by standardizing identity governance processes, ensuring that user access is consistently enforced according to security policies. Automated compliance dashboards provide security teams with real-time visibility into identity-related risks, enabling rapid incident response to policy violations. IAM automation also facilitates periodic access certification reviews, ensuring that organizations maintain accurate records of user entitlements and eliminate unnecessary privileges that could lead to compliance gaps.

Privileged access management (PAM) automation is critical for ensuring compliance with regulatory frameworks that mandate strict control over high-risk accounts. Traditional privileged access models rely on manual access approvals, leading to delays and potential security oversights. IAM automation enhances PAM security by enforcing just-in-time (JIT) access provisioning, granting privileged users temporary administrative permissions only when necessary. Automated PAM solutions integrate with compliance policies to ensure that privileged access requests follow strict approval workflows, enforce session recording, and generate audit logs for forensic investigations. Compliance frameworks such as SOX and ISO 27001 require organizations to monitor and document privileged access activities, and IAM automation simplifies this process by providing detailed visibility into all privileged account interactions.

Third-party identity governance automation is essential for organizations that grant external vendors, contractors, and business partners access to corporate resources. Regulatory frameworks mandate that organizations enforce strict authentication and authorization policies for third-party users, ensuring that external entities do not retain unnecessary privileges. IAM automation enforces temporary access policies for third-party accounts, automatically revoking access upon contract expiration or project completion. Continuous monitoring of third-party authentication logs enables organizations to detect policy violations and enforce remediation actions in real time. By automating third-party identity governance, organizations can ensure compliance with security regulations while reducing the risk of supply chain attacks.

IAM compliance automation enhances security monitoring by integrating with Security Information and Event Management (SIEM) solutions to provide real-time detection of identity-related threats. Automated IAM solutions generate compliance reports that document authentication failures, privilege escalations, and access anomalies, ensuring that security teams can respond to threats proactively. Regulatory audits require organizations to maintain detailed logs of access activities, and IAM automation simplifies compliance reporting by generating preconfigured reports that align with industry standards. Automated compliance dashboards enable security teams to track identity governance metrics, detect policy violations, and enforce corrective actions without manual intervention.

Employee access training and awareness automation ensures that users understand compliance policies and security best practices. Organizations must educate employees on secure authentication methods, phishing risks, and identity governance responsibilities to maintain compliance with regulatory frameworks. IAM automation reinforces security awareness by requiring users to complete periodic compliance training, acknowledge security policies during login sessions, and adhere to MFA authentication requirements. Automated security alerts notify users of potential compliance violations, ensuring that employees follow best practices for secure access management.

IAM automation plays a crucial role in streamlining compliance audits by providing regulators with structured evidence of policy enforcement. Organizations that rely on manual compliance tracking often struggle with audit readiness, as access certifications, privilege reviews, and authentication logs must be reviewed manually. IAM automation eliminates this challenge by maintaining real-time audit trails that document all identity-related activities. Compliance automation tools generate detailed access reports, tracking user entitlements, policy violations, and remediation actions taken to enforce compliance. By automating compliance controls, organizations reduce audit preparation time, improve regulatory adherence, and enhance overall security governance.

Automating compliance controls in IAM ensures that security policies are consistently enforced, regulatory mandates are met, and access risks are minimized. By leveraging IAM automation for access provisioning, privileged access management, third-party identity governance, and compliance reporting, organizations can achieve continuous regulatory adherence while reducing administrative overhead. Implementing automated compliance controls strengthens identity security, prevents unauthorized access, and provides organizations with the necessary tools to maintain audit readiness across complex IT environments.

Security Information and Event Management (SIEM) for IAM Audits

Security Information and Event Management (SIEM) plays a crucial role in Identity and Access Management (IAM) audits by providing organizations with real-time monitoring, log correlation, threat detection, and compliance reporting. SIEM solutions aggregate and analyze security events from various sources, including authentication systems, access controls, privileged account activities, and identity governance tools. Regulatory frameworks such as SOX, GDPR, HIPAA, NIST, and ISO 27001 require organizations to implement logging and monitoring mechanisms that ensure access controls are enforced, identity-related threats are detected, and compliance requirements are met. By integrating SIEM with IAM systems, organizations can enhance security visibility, detect policy violations, and generate audit-ready reports.

IAM audits require organizations to maintain comprehensive logs that track authentication attempts, user access requests, privilege escalations, and account modifications. SIEM solutions centralize these logs, enabling security teams to correlate identity-related events across multiple systems. The Sarbanes-Oxley Act (SOX) mandates strict access control and auditing requirements for financial systems, requiring organizations to monitor user activities that could impact financial integrity. SIEM solutions support SOX compliance by tracking login attempts, unauthorized access attempts, and changes to financial records. Automated SIEM reports provide auditors with evidence of IAM policy enforcement, ensuring that financial data remains protected from insider threats and unauthorized modifications.

The General Data Protection Regulation (GDPR) enforces strict data access and privacy controls, requiring organizations to monitor and log all access to personally identifiable information (PII). SIEM enhances GDPR compliance by aggregating access logs from IAM systems, enabling organizations to detect unauthorized access attempts and policy violations. Real-time alerts generated by SIEM solutions notify security teams of suspicious IAM activities, such as failed authentication attempts, abnormal login locations, or privilege escalations involving customer data. Organizations must retain authentication logs for a predefined period to demonstrate compliance with GDPR's audit requirements. By integrating SIEM with IAM systems, organizations can streamline access monitoring, enforce security policies, and provide regulators with clear evidence of data protection measures.

HIPAA requires healthcare organizations to implement security measures that protect electronic protected health information (ePHI). SIEM supports HIPAA compliance by collecting and analyzing authentication logs, access requests, and privileged account activities associated with ePHI. Healthcare organizations must ensure that only authorized personnel access patient records and that any unauthorized access attempts are promptly identified. SIEM solutions detect unusual access patterns, such as excessive login failures, access from unrecognized devices, or unauthorized attempts to modify patient data. By maintaining an audit trail of all IAM-related activities, SIEM solutions help healthcare organizations demonstrate compliance with HIPAA security rules and prevent identity-related security incidents.

NIST guidelines emphasize the importance of real-time monitoring and threat detection for IAM security. SIEM aligns with NIST recommendations by providing continuous log correlation, anomaly detection, and forensic analysis capabilities. Organizations implementing NIST-compliant IAM policies must ensure that access events, authentication failures, and privilege changes are monitored in real time. SIEM solutions use behavioral analytics to identify deviations from normal user behavior, flagging potential security threats such as account takeovers or credential-based attacks. By leveraging SIEM for IAM audits, organizations can enhance incident response, prevent identity fraud, and maintain compliance with federal cybersecurity standards.

ISO 27001 mandates that organizations maintain an Information

Security Management System (ISMS) that includes logging, monitoring, and access control enforcement. SIEM supports ISO 27001 compliance by providing centralized visibility into IAM activities, ensuring that security teams can track access logs, detect unauthorized privilege changes, and respond to security incidents in real time. Organizations must implement security controls that prevent privilege escalation, unauthorized account modifications, and identity-based attacks. SIEM automation enhances ISO 27001 compliance by generating security reports, monitoring IAM logs for compliance violations, and providing audit trails that document all access-related events.

Privileged Access Management (PAM) integration with SIEM enhances security by ensuring that administrative account activities are continuously monitored and audited. Privileged accounts have elevated access to critical systems, making them high-risk targets for cyberattacks and insider threats. SIEM solutions aggregate privileged access logs, tracking administrative login attempts, session activities, and privilege modifications. Compliance frameworks require organizations to enforce strict monitoring of privileged accounts, ensuring that unauthorized privilege escalations are detected and investigated. SIEM dashboards provide security teams with real-time visibility into privileged account activities, allowing them to respond to suspicious behavior and enforce compliance policies effectively.

Multi-cloud and hybrid IAM environments present additional security and compliance challenges, as organizations must monitor access across multiple platforms and providers. SIEM centralizes IAM logs from cloud-based identity providers, on-premises authentication systems, and third-party applications, ensuring that organizations can track identity-related security events across their entire infrastructure. Compliance regulations require organizations to enforce consistent access controls across cloud environments, preventing unauthorized data exposure. SIEM solutions help organizations monitor cloud IAM policies, detect misconfigurations, and enforce real-time security controls that align with regulatory requirements. By integrating SIEM with cloud IAM frameworks such as AWS IAM, Azure AD, and Google Cloud IAM, organizations can ensure compliance across their entire identity ecosystem.

Third-party identity governance is another critical compliance consideration for IAM audits. Organizations frequently grant vendors, contractors, and external partners access to internal systems, increasing security risks. SIEM solutions help enforce compliance by tracking third-party authentication events, access privileges, and session activities. Regulatory frameworks require organizations to monitor third-party access continuously, ensuring that external users do not retain excessive permissions beyond their contractual engagement. SIEM automation enables organizations to detect unauthorized third-party access attempts, enforce time-limited access policies, and generate compliance reports that document external user activities. By integrating SIEM with third-party IAM controls, organizations can mitigate supply chain security risks and ensure regulatory adherence.

IAM compliance automation with SIEM enhances security monitoring by reducing false positives, detecting real threats faster, and automating compliance reporting. Organizations must generate IAM audit reports that demonstrate adherence to regulatory mandates, detailing user authentication patterns, policy enforcement metrics, and access review findings. SIEM dashboards provide real-time compliance insights, enabling security teams to track IAM governance metrics, detect policy violations, and enforce corrective actions without manual intervention. Automated IAM compliance reports generated by SIEM solutions help organizations prepare for regulatory audits, reducing administrative overhead while ensuring continuous compliance monitoring.

User awareness and IAM security training programs benefit from SIEM integration by providing security teams with insights into authentication trends, access anomalies, and policy violations. Organizations must educate employees on secure authentication practices, privilege management responsibilities, and compliance obligations. SIEM solutions reinforce security training by identifying risky user behaviors, enforcing security awareness assessments, and providing real-time policy enforcement alerts. Strengthening IAM security awareness helps organizations prevent identity-based security incidents and maintain compliance with regulatory frameworks.

Security Information and Event Management (SIEM) solutions are essential for IAM audits, providing real-time monitoring, threat detection, and compliance reporting. By integrating SIEM with IAM, PAM, and identity governance solutions, organizations can centralize access log management, detect identity-based security threats, and automate compliance enforcement. SIEM enhances regulatory compliance by ensuring continuous identity monitoring, generating audit-ready reports, and enforcing security policies that align with SOX, GDPR, HIPAA, NIST, and ISO 27001 requirements.

Managing Orphan Accounts and Compliance Risks

Orphan accounts represent a significant security and compliance risk in Identity and Access Management (IAM). These accounts, which remain active after an employee, contractor, or third-party user leaves an organization, create opportunities for unauthorized access, privilege abuse, and insider threats. Regulatory frameworks such as SOX, GDPR, HIPAA, NIST, and ISO 27001 require organizations to implement strict access control policies that prevent orphan accounts from accumulating and ensure timely deprovisioning. Failure to manage orphan accounts effectively can result in compliance violations, data breaches, and security incidents that expose sensitive information to unauthorized users.

One of the primary causes of orphan accounts is the lack of automated identity lifecycle management. When organizations rely on manual access provisioning and deprovisioning processes, user accounts may not be properly revoked after an employee's departure. This issue is especially prevalent in organizations with high workforce turnover, complex IT environments, and multiple identity repositories. IAM automation reduces this risk by ensuring that user accounts are immediately deactivated or removed when an employee resigns, is terminated, or transitions to a different role. Automating deprovisioning eliminates human error, enforces compliance policies, and ensures that orphan accounts do not persist in the system.

SOX compliance mandates that organizations enforce strict access control mechanisms to protect financial data from unauthorized modifications. Orphan accounts pose a direct risk to SOX compliance, as they provide an entry point for attackers to access financial reporting systems undetected. Organizations subject to SOX regulations must implement automated user lifecycle management, enforce access review policies, and maintain audit trails that track account deactivation processes. Regular IAM audits help identify orphan accounts associated with former employees, ensuring that access permissions are revoked promptly to prevent financial fraud and insider threats.

The General Data Protection Regulation (GDPR) enforces strict data access policies to protect personally identifiable information (PII) from unauthorized exposure. Orphan accounts that retain access to customer data violate GDPR's security and privacy requirements, increasing the risk of non-compliance penalties. Organizations must ensure that all user accounts associated with personal data processing are deactivated when no longer needed. IAM solutions help enforce GDPR compliance by integrating with human resources (HR) systems to trigger automatic account deprovisioning upon employee termination. By regularly auditing orphan accounts and ensuring that inactive accounts do not retain access to PII, organizations can align IAM policies with GDPR compliance requirements.

HIPAA mandates that healthcare organizations implement security measures to protect electronic protected health information (ePHI). Orphan accounts in healthcare environments create compliance risks by allowing unauthorized access to patient records, medical billing systems, and prescription databases. HIPAA requires organizations to conduct periodic access reviews to detect and remove orphan accounts associated with former employees, contractors, and medical staff. IAM automation helps healthcare providers enforce HIPAA compliance by implementing automated account termination workflows, privileged access revocation, and continuous monitoring of inactive user accounts. Detecting and mitigating orphan accounts ensures that ePHI remains protected from unauthorized access and insider threats.

NIST guidelines emphasize the importance of continuous identity governance and access control enforcement to mitigate cybersecurity risks. Orphan accounts violate NIST security principles by providing attackers with an opportunity to exploit unused credentials for lateral movement, privilege escalation, and data exfiltration. Organizations following NIST standards must implement IAM policies that enforce automatic deprovisioning, regularly audit inactive accounts, and integrate IAM systems with security monitoring tools such as Security

Information and Event Management (SIEM) solutions. By detecting and eliminating orphan accounts, organizations strengthen IAM security and ensure compliance with NIST cybersecurity frameworks.

ISO 27001 requires organizations to maintain an Information Security Management System (ISMS) that includes strict access control policies to prevent unauthorized system access. Orphan accounts undermine ISO 27001 compliance by increasing the likelihood of unauthorized access to corporate data, cloud resources, and privileged systems. Organizations must implement automated IAM solutions that track user identity status, enforce role-based access control (RBAC), and generate audit reports that document orphan account remediation efforts. IAM governance frameworks integrated with ISO 27001 compliance ensure that orphan accounts are continuously monitored, reviewed, and removed from all identity repositories.

Privileged orphan accounts pose an even greater security and compliance risk due to their elevated access to critical IT systems, databases, and administrative functions. These accounts, if left active after an administrator or privileged user departs, provide attackers with an opportunity to bypass security controls and execute unauthorized changes. Regulatory frameworks require organizations to enforce Privileged Access Management (PAM) policies that detect and deactivate orphaned privileged accounts in real time. Implementing just-in-time (JIT) access provisioning ensures that privileged accounts are only activated when required, preventing them from becoming orphaned over time. Organizations must integrate PAM with IAM solutions to continuously monitor privileged account activity and ensure compliance with SOX, HIPAA, and ISO 27001 security standards.

Third-party vendor accounts also contribute to orphan account risks, as contractors and external service providers often receive temporary access to corporate systems. Organizations must enforce strict third-party identity governance policies to ensure that external users do not retain system access beyond their contractual engagements. Compliance frameworks mandate that organizations regularly review and revoke third-party access, ensuring that orphan accounts associated with vendors are deactivated upon project completion. IAM automation helps organizations enforce third-party compliance by implementing time-limited access controls, monitoring external account activity, and generating reports that track vendor authentication attempts.

IAM audit processes play a crucial role in identifying and mitigating orphan accounts. Organizations must implement periodic access reviews that assess user account activity, detect inactive accounts, and trigger automated deprovisioning workflows. Compliance frameworks require organizations to maintain audit logs that track access revocations, ensuring that security teams can verify IAM policy enforcement. Integrating IAM audits with SIEM solutions enhances compliance monitoring by detecting orphan accounts in real time, generating alerts for unapproved account activity, and enforcing remediation actions to align with regulatory requirements.

IAM training and awareness programs support orphan account management by educating employees, security teams, and IT administrators on compliance responsibilities and access control best practices. Organizations must enforce security policies that require employees to notify HR and IAM teams of departures, role changes, or contract terminations to ensure timely access revocation. IAM solutions can reinforce security awareness by displaying compliance reminders, requiring policy acknowledgments during authentication, and integrating security training modules that address orphan account risks. Strengthening IAM awareness reduces the likelihood of compliance violations and improves identity governance effectiveness.

Managing orphan accounts and compliance risks requires organizations to implement automated IAM policies, enforce continuous identity governance, and integrate compliance monitoring tools. By proactively detecting and deactivating orphan accounts, organizations enhance security, prevent unauthorized access, and maintain compliance with SOX, GDPR, HIPAA, NIST, and ISO 27001 regulatory requirements. IAM automation, privileged access management, third-party identity governance, and periodic access reviews ensure that orphan accounts do not persist in IT environments, reducing compliance risks and strengthening IAM security.

Continuous Monitoring for IAM Compliance

Continuous monitoring in Identity and Access Management (IAM) is essential for ensuring that access controls, authentication policies, and identity governance measures remain aligned with regulatory compliance requirements. Frameworks such as SOX, GDPR, HIPAA, NIST, and ISO 27001 mandate that organizations implement real-time monitoring mechanisms to detect unauthorized access, prevent security breaches, and maintain audit readiness. Without continuous monitoring, organizations face increased risks of insider threats, credential-based attacks, and privilege misuse, which can result in compliance violations and regulatory penalties.

IAM compliance requires organizations to maintain strict access control policies that define how user identities are provisioned, authenticated, and monitored across IT environments. Traditional periodic access reviews are not sufficient to address evolving security risks, as unauthorized access attempts can occur at any time. Continuous monitoring enhances compliance by providing real-time visibility into user activities, detecting anomalies, and enforcing policy-based security controls. IAM solutions integrated with Security Information and Event Management (SIEM) platforms enable organizations to collect and analyze authentication logs, privilege escalation attempts, and account modification events, ensuring that suspicious behavior is promptly identified and mitigated.

SOX compliance mandates that organizations protect financial systems by monitoring access to sensitive financial data and enforcing least privilege access policies. Continuous IAM monitoring supports SOX compliance by tracking login attempts, failed authentication attempts, and unauthorized access to financial reporting systems. Organizations must implement real-time alerts that notify security teams of policy violations, such as excessive failed login attempts or unauthorized changes to user roles. By integrating IAM monitoring with automated remediation workflows, organizations can enforce corrective actions immediately, preventing fraudulent activities that could impact financial integrity.

The General Data Protection Regulation (GDPR) enforces strict access control policies to ensure that personal data remains protected from unauthorized access and exposure. Continuous IAM monitoring enhances GDPR compliance by tracking user access to personally identifiable information (PII), ensuring that only authorized users interact with customer data. IAM solutions generate real-time compliance reports that document data access patterns, flag unauthorized authentication attempts, and trigger alerts for anomalous activity. Organizations must also enforce real-time session monitoring, ensuring that data processing activities comply with GDPR requirements and that unauthorized access attempts are blocked before they result in data breaches.

HIPAA requires healthcare organizations to implement security measures that protect electronic protected health information (ePHI). Continuous IAM monitoring plays a critical role in HIPAA compliance by tracking user interactions with patient records, enforcing role-based access control (RBAC), and preventing unauthorized privilege escalations. Real-time monitoring solutions detect suspicious behavior, such as attempts to access patient records outside of approved work hours, and generate compliance reports that document security policy enforcement. Organizations must also monitor privileged user activities, ensuring that administrative access to healthcare systems is logged, reviewed, and restricted based on HIPAA security rules.

NIST guidelines emphasize the importance of real-time monitoring for IAM compliance, requiring organizations to implement continuous authentication, anomaly detection, and identity risk assessments. IAM monitoring under NIST frameworks involves tracking user access events, detecting behavioral deviations, and enforcing risk-based authentication (RBA). Organizations must integrate IAM monitoring with behavioral analytics tools that assess login trends, device trust levels, and session durations to identify high-risk activities.

Continuous IAM monitoring ensures that organizations can respond to identity-based security incidents in real time, reducing the risk of credential-based attacks and unauthorized access attempts.

ISO 27001 mandates that organizations implement an Information Security Management System (ISMS) that includes continuous access monitoring and identity governance controls. IAM monitoring supports ISO 27001 compliance by enforcing automated access reviews, detecting security policy violations, and generating compliance audit reports. Organizations must implement IAM monitoring policies that define how user activities are logged, how authentication attempts are analyzed, and how security incidents are escalated. By leveraging continuous monitoring tools, organizations can proactively identify security gaps, enforce compliance controls, and maintain adherence to ISO 27001 access control requirements.

Privileged access monitoring is a key component of continuous IAM monitoring, ensuring that administrative users do not misuse their elevated permissions. Compliance frameworks require organizations to enforce privileged session monitoring, logging all administrative activities, and detecting unauthorized privilege escalations. IAM solutions integrated with Privileged Access Management (PAM) platforms provide real-time visibility into privileged account activities, ensuring that administrators do not retain excessive permissions beyond necessary job functions. Continuous monitoring of privileged accounts prevents unauthorized changes to critical systems, enhances accountability, and reduces compliance risks associated with privilege abuse.

Multi-cloud and hybrid IAM environments introduce additional monitoring challenges, as organizations must track user activities across multiple cloud platforms, identity providers, and third-party applications. Continuous monitoring solutions provide centralized visibility into cloud-based IAM events, ensuring that access control policies remain consistent across AWS, Microsoft Azure, Google Cloud, and on-premises infrastructure. Compliance regulations require organizations to enforce security monitoring for cloud-based

IAM policies, ensuring that unauthorized access attempts, privilege modifications, and identity misconfigurations are promptly detected and remediated. By integrating continuous monitoring with cloud IAM frameworks, organizations maintain compliance while preventing cloud-based security incidents.

Third-party access monitoring is another critical IAM compliance requirement, as organizations frequently grant external vendors, contractors, and business partners temporary access to internal systems. Continuous IAM monitoring ensures that third-party authentication attempts, access requests, and session activities are tracked in real time, preventing unauthorized data access. Regulatory frameworks require organizations to implement third-party identity governance policies that define how external accounts are provisioned, monitored, and deactivated when no longer needed. IAM monitoring solutions detect anomalies in third-party access patterns, triggering security alerts for suspicious behavior and enforcing compliance with strict authentication policies.

IAM automation enhances continuous monitoring by reducing manual oversight, detecting threats faster, and streamlining compliance reporting. Organizations must implement automated identity risk assessments that analyze authentication logs, detect access anomalies, and enforce real-time remediation actions. Compliance frameworks require organizations to generate IAM audit reports that document access patterns, privilege escalations, and policy enforcement metrics. Automated IAM compliance dashboards provide security teams with real-time insights into access control effectiveness, enabling proactive compliance enforcement and rapid incident response.

Security awareness and IAM training programs benefit from continuous monitoring by providing organizations with data-driven insights into user authentication behavior, policy violations, and security risks. Organizations must educate employees on secure access practices, authentication best practices, and compliance obligations. IAM solutions integrate continuous monitoring with security awareness programs, displaying real-time compliance notifications, enforcing periodic access policy acknowledgments, and requiring security training assessments. Strengthening security awareness ensures that employees follow IAM policies, reducing compliance violations and mitigating identity-based security threats.

Continuous IAM monitoring enhances security visibility, enforces compliance policies, and prevents unauthorized access attempts. By integrating IAM monitoring with SIEM, PAM, and identity analytics tools, organizations can track authentication events, detect anomalies, and maintain compliance with SOX, GDPR, HIPAA, NIST, and ISO 27001 regulatory requirements. IAM automation enables real-time compliance monitoring, streamlining security operations while ensuring that identity governance policies remain effective across complex IT environments.

Access Recertification and Periodic Reviews

Access recertification and periodic reviews are critical components of Identity and Access Management (IAM) compliance, ensuring that users retain only the necessary permissions for their job functions. Regulatory frameworks such as SOX, GDPR, HIPAA, NIST, and ISO 27001 mandate that organizations perform regular reviews of access rights to prevent privilege creep, unauthorized access, and security violations. By implementing structured access recertification processes, organizations can maintain compliance, enhance security, and reduce the risk of insider threats and credential-based attacks.

IAM systems assign user access based on predefined roles, responsibilities, and business needs. However, over time, employees may accumulate excessive privileges due to role changes, project assignments, or temporary access grants. If not periodically reviewed and adjusted, these accumulated permissions can lead to security vulnerabilities and compliance violations. Access recertification ensures that managers, security teams, and auditors systematically review user entitlements, validate their necessity, and revoke unnecessary permissions. Automated IAM solutions streamline access certification by triggering periodic reviews, generating audit reports, and enforcing corrective actions based on compliance policies.

SOX compliance requires organizations to enforce strict access controls for financial systems, preventing unauthorized modifications to financial data. Periodic access reviews help organizations identify excessive permissions that could be exploited for fraudulent activities, such as unauthorized financial transactions or data manipulation. Organizations subject to SOX regulations must document access review findings, track role modifications, and maintain audit trails that demonstrate continuous access governance. IAM automation enhances SOX compliance by scheduling access reviews at regular intervals, enforcing approval workflows, and revoking access when business justifications are no longer valid.

The General Data Protection Regulation (GDPR) mandates that organizations enforce data access restrictions to protect personally identifiable information (PII). Access recertification ensures that only authorized personnel have access to customer data, reducing the risk of data breaches and non-compliance penalties. IAM solutions generate access certification reports that document who has access to PII, why access is granted, and whether it is still necessary. GDPR compliance audits require organizations to present evidence of access control enforcement, making periodic reviews an essential part of IAM governance. Automated access recertification workflows reduce manual review efforts, ensuring that data access remains aligned with regulatory requirements.

HIPAA enforces strict access control policies to protect electronic protected health information (ePHI). Healthcare organizations must conduct periodic access reviews to validate that doctors, nurses, and administrative staff have the appropriate level of access to patient records. Over-provisioned access to ePHI increases the risk of data breaches, insider threats, and non-compliance penalties. IAM automation supports HIPAA compliance by generating real-time access review dashboards, tracking user access to medical data, and enforcing revocation policies for excessive permissions. Automated access certification ensures that healthcare organizations maintain strict access governance while reducing the administrative burden of manual reviews.

NIST guidelines emphasize the importance of periodic access reviews to enforce least privilege access, detect policy violations, and prevent privilege escalation attacks. Organizations following NIST cybersecurity frameworks must establish structured access recertification processes that track user entitlements, assess risk levels, and enforce remediation actions. IAM automation enhances NIST compliance by integrating machine learning-based risk analysis, detecting anomalous access patterns, and enforcing time-sensitive access revocation. Continuous monitoring of access reviews ensures that IAM policies remain effective and that unauthorized privilege accumulation is prevented before it leads to security incidents.

ISO 27001 requires organizations to implement an Information Security Management System (ISMS) that includes periodic access certification and review processes. Organizations must document access control policies, perform regular entitlement reviews, and generate compliance reports that demonstrate IAM policy enforcement. ISO 27001 audits require organizations to validate that users, third-party vendors, and privileged accounts do not retain excessive permissions beyond their job requirements. IAM automation simplifies ISO 27001 compliance by scheduling periodic access reviews, enforcing approval workflows, and providing real-time audit logs that track user access modifications.

Privileged access recertification is a critical security measure for enforcing compliance and preventing privilege abuse. Privileged accounts, such as system administrators, database managers, and IT security personnel, have elevated permissions that could be exploited if not properly managed. Periodic privileged access reviews ensure that administrative users do not retain excessive permissions that increase security risks. Compliance frameworks require organizations to monitor and document privileged access activities, ensuring that unauthorized privilege escalations are detected and remediated. IAM automation enforces just-in-time (JIT) privileged access provisioning, granting temporary administrative privileges based on business needs and automatically revoking them after task completion.

Third-party access recertification ensures that external vendors, contractors, and business partners do not retain unnecessary access to corporate resources. Regulatory frameworks mandate that organizations enforce strict access controls for third-party users, preventing unauthorized access to sensitive systems. Periodic access reviews ensure that third-party accounts are continuously evaluated, deactivated when no longer needed, and monitored for security risks. IAM automation enhances third-party access governance by enforcing time-restricted access policies, generating real-time access review reports, and integrating with vendor identity management systems to ensure compliance with regulatory mandates.

IAM audit processes play a crucial role in access recertification by providing organizations with visibility into user access trends, policy violations, and remediation actions. Security teams must review access certification reports, analyze entitlement change logs, and enforce corrective measures to align with compliance requirements. IAM automation enhances audit readiness by generating detailed access review reports that document certification outcomes, access revocations, and policy adjustments. Compliance audits require organizations to demonstrate continuous identity governance, making periodic access reviews an essential part of IAM risk management.

IAM security awareness and training programs support access recertification by educating employees, managers, and IT administrators on compliance responsibilities and access governance best practices. Organizations must enforce security training policies that require users to complete periodic IAM awareness assessments, acknowledge access control policies, and follow least privilege access principles. IAM solutions reinforce security training by displaying policy reminders during access certification workflows, enforcing compliance acknowledgments, and tracking user participation in security training programs. Strengthening IAM awareness ensures that employees understand the importance of access recertification and follow security policies effectively.

Access recertification and periodic reviews are essential for maintaining IAM compliance, preventing privilege accumulation, and enforcing least privilege access controls. By integrating IAM automation, privileged access management, third-party identity governance, and continuous monitoring solutions, organizations can streamline access certification, detect policy violations, and reduce security risks. Regulatory frameworks such as SOX, GDPR, HIPAA, NIST, and ISO 27001 require organizations to enforce structured access recertification processes, ensuring that access privileges are regularly reviewed, justified, and revoked when necessary. Implementing automated access recertification workflows strengthens IAM governance, enhances compliance enforcement, and mitigates the risks associated with excessive user permissions.

Data Retention and Identity Management Regulations

Data retention policies play a critical role in Identity and Access Management (IAM) compliance, ensuring that organizations manage identity-related data in accordance with regulatory requirements. Various regulations, including SOX, GDPR, HIPAA, NIST, and ISO 27001, mandate how long identity records, authentication logs, access control data, and user activity logs must be stored. Failure to comply with these data retention policies can lead to compliance violations, data security risks, and legal consequences. Organizations must implement IAM strategies that define clear data retention periods, enforce secure storage policies, and automate data disposal when records are no longer required.

IAM data retention policies govern the lifecycle of identity-related information, including user authentication records, login attempts, access logs, privilege assignments, and identity verification details. These records are essential for auditing, forensic investigations, and regulatory compliance verification. However, different regulations impose varying retention requirements, making it necessary for organizations to align IAM data retention policies with specific legal mandates. Automated IAM solutions ensure that data is retained for the required duration while enforcing secure deletion mechanisms to prevent unauthorized access to outdated identity records.

SOX compliance mandates that financial institutions retain records related to system access, authentication logs, and privileged user activities for a minimum period. Organizations subject to SOX regulations must maintain audit trails that track changes to financial systems, ensuring that all access attempts, approvals, and modifications are documented. IAM solutions automate SOX compliance by enforcing retention policies that securely store authentication logs, generate access review reports, and archive identity management records based on financial auditing requirements. Implementing strict IAM data retention policies ensures that organizations remain compliant with SOX auditing standards while preventing unauthorized access to financial data.

The General Data Protection Regulation (GDPR) enforces strict data retention policies to protect personal data and limit unnecessary data storage. Organizations must ensure that identity-related information, including authentication logs and access records, is retained only for as long as necessary to fulfill legal or business requirements. GDPR requires organizations to implement data minimization principles, ensuring that IAM systems do not retain user data beyond the required retention period. Automated IAM compliance solutions enforce GDPR retention policies by regularly purging outdated identity records, encrypting stored data, and ensuring that authentication logs comply with GDPR's right-to-be-forgotten mandate. Organizations must also document identity data retention policies and demonstrate compliance during GDPR audits.

HIPAA mandates that healthcare organizations retain electronic protected health information (ePHI) access logs and authentication records for a specific period to ensure patient data security and regulatory compliance. Healthcare providers must store IAM-related data such as login attempts, session activity logs, and privileged access records in a secure manner to prevent unauthorized access to patient information. HIPAA compliance audits review IAM data retention policies to verify that identity records are securely stored and properly disposed of after the required retention period. IAM automation ensures that healthcare organizations enforce HIPAA retention policies by monitoring access to patient records, generating compliance reports, and applying secure deletion procedures when identity records expire.

NIST guidelines emphasize the importance of maintaining identity and authentication records for security monitoring, forensic investigations, and incident response. Organizations following NIST cybersecurity frameworks must enforce IAM data retention policies that define how long authentication logs, failed login attempts, and user access histories are stored. SIEM (Security Information and Event

Management) solutions integrated with IAM platforms help organizations retain identity logs, detect security anomalies, and generate audit trails for compliance verification. NIST-aligned IAM retention policies ensure that organizations can analyze authentication trends, prevent identity-related security incidents, and maintain regulatory adherence.

ISO 27001 requires organizations to implement an Information Security Management System (ISMS) that includes structured data retention policies for identity management records. Organizations must define how long authentication logs, access control records, and privilege assignment data are retained to comply with ISO 27001's security monitoring and auditing requirements. IAM solutions enforce ISO 27001 retention policies by categorizing identity records based on risk levels, applying encryption to stored authentication logs, and automating log retention expiration policies. Secure identity data disposal methods, such as cryptographic wiping and secure deletion protocols, ensure that IAM records are permanently removed when retention periods expire.

Privileged access retention policies are critical for ensuring compliance with regulatory frameworks that mandate strict control over high-risk accounts. Organizations must store privileged account activity logs, administrative session recordings, and access approvals for a defined period to ensure auditability. Regulatory compliance requires organizations to maintain detailed logs of privileged access requests, just-in-time (JIT) privilege grants, and privilege escalations to prevent unauthorized administrative actions. IAM automation enforces privileged access retention policies by securely archiving administrative session logs, monitoring privileged account activities, and applying access review procedures to ensure compliance with SOX, HIPAA, and ISO 27001 standards.

Third-party identity management retention policies ensure that vendor access records, contractor authentication logs, and partner identity data are stored securely for compliance verification. Regulatory frameworks require organizations to monitor and retain third-party authentication records to prevent unauthorized access and track identity governance compliance. IAM solutions enforce retention policies by integrating with third-party identity providers, maintaining access logs for external users, and applying automatic expiration rules to revoke access and delete outdated third-party credentials. Ensuring compliance with third-party retention policies reduces supply chain security risks and strengthens IAM data governance.

IAM audit processes play a key role in verifying compliance with identity data retention policies. Organizations must conduct periodic IAM audits that assess data retention practices, review identity storage policies, and validate secure deletion procedures. Compliance frameworks require organizations to maintain documentation that details IAM retention schedules, data protection mechanisms, and secure disposal workflows. Automated IAM compliance tools generate audit-ready reports that summarize identity data retention activities, track log expiration timelines, and ensure that retention policies align with regulatory mandates.

IAM security awareness and training programs support data retention compliance by educating employees, administrators, and security teams on identity data protection responsibilities. Organizations must enforce training policies that require users to follow IAM retention guidelines, acknowledge security policies, and complete periodic compliance assessments. IAM solutions reinforce security training by displaying data retention policy reminders, enforcing policy acknowledgments during authentication, and tracking user participation in security training programs. Strengthening IAM awareness ensures that employees understand data retention compliance requirements and follow best practices for secure identity record management.

Data retention and identity management regulations require organizations to enforce strict storage, access, and deletion policies for identity-related information. By implementing automated IAM compliance solutions, privileged access governance controls, and third-party identity retention policies, organizations can ensure compliance with SOX, GDPR, HIPAA, NIST, and ISO 27001 standards. IAM automation streamlines data retention enforcement, reduces compliance risks, and ensures that identity records are securely managed throughout their lifecycle.

Handling Insider Threats and IAM Compliance Measures

Insider threats pose a significant security and compliance risk to organizations, as they involve individuals with legitimate access to sensitive systems, data, and applications. Unlike external cyber threats, insider threats originate from employees, contractors, or business partners who misuse their access privileges for malicious purposes or due to negligence. Regulatory frameworks such as SOX, GDPR, HIPAA, NIST, and ISO 27001 require organizations to implement strict Identity and Access Management (IAM) controls to mitigate the risks associated with insider threats. By enforcing access governance policies, monitoring user activities, and implementing privileged access controls, organizations can detect, prevent, and respond to insider threats while ensuring compliance with regulatory mandates.

IAM plays a crucial role in limiting insider threats by enforcing least privilege access policies. Users should only have access to the resources required to perform their job functions, reducing the likelihood of privilege misuse. Role-based access control (RBAC) and attribute-based access control (ABAC) models ensure that users receive permissions based on predefined policies and contextual factors. IAM solutions automatically adjust access rights as employees change roles or responsibilities, preventing privilege accumulation over time. Regulatory frameworks mandate strict enforcement of least privilege policies, ensuring that insider threats are minimized by restricting unnecessary access to critical systems and sensitive data.

SOX compliance requires organizations to enforce strong access controls for financial systems to prevent unauthorized modifications and fraudulent activities. Insider threats within financial institutions can lead to financial fraud, unauthorized data manipulation, and non-compliance with SOX auditing standards. IAM solutions enhance SOX compliance by tracking all access attempts to financial records, enforcing multi-factor authentication (MFA) for privileged accounts, and generating audit trails that document user interactions with financial data. Continuous monitoring of IAM logs enables security teams to detect suspicious insider activities, such as unauthorized privilege escalations or repeated failed login attempts, ensuring that insider threats are identified before they cause financial harm.

The General Data Protection Regulation (GDPR) enforces strict access control and data protection measures to prevent unauthorized access to personally identifiable information (PII). Insider threats pose a direct risk to GDPR compliance, as employees with excessive permissions can expose customer data, either intentionally or accidentally. IAM compliance measures such as real-time user activity monitoring, data masking, and automated access reviews ensure that insiders do not retain unnecessary access to customer information. Organizations must implement security policies that require logging all access attempts to PII, ensuring that any unauthorized actions are immediately detected and mitigated. GDPR mandates that organizations report data breaches caused by insider threats within a specified timeframe, making continuous IAM monitoring essential for regulatory adherence.

HIPAA compliance requires healthcare organizations to protect electronic protected health information (ePHI) from unauthorized access, including insider threats from medical staff, administrative personnel, and IT administrators. IAM compliance measures ensure that access to ePHI is strictly controlled, logged, and reviewed periodically. Privileged access management (PAM) solutions prevent excessive permissions for healthcare employees, enforcing session recording and automatic privilege revocation after a defined period. IAM automation detects suspicious user behavior, such as unauthorized attempts to access patient records outside normal work hours, ensuring that insider threats are addressed in real time. HIPAA audits require organizations to provide detailed IAM reports that document access control enforcement, making continuous monitoring and auditing critical components of compliance.

NIST guidelines emphasize the importance of insider threat detection, continuous authentication, and real-time security monitoring.

Organizations implementing NIST cybersecurity frameworks must integrate IAM solutions with behavioral analytics tools that detect anomalies in user access patterns. Machine learning-based IAM solutions assess risk levels based on user behavior, triggering security alerts for deviations from normal activity. By enforcing risk-based authentication (RBA), organizations can challenge users with additional verification steps when suspicious behavior is detected. NIST-aligned IAM policies ensure that insider threats are mitigated through continuous identity validation, least privilege enforcement, and real-time monitoring of privileged accounts.

ISO 27001 requires organizations to implement an Information Security Management System (ISMS) that includes strict IAM policies to prevent insider threats. Access control enforcement, periodic access reviews, and privileged session monitoring are key IAM compliance measures for ISO 27001 certification. Organizations must maintain detailed access logs, ensuring that all user activities are traceable and auditable. IAM automation enhances ISO 27001 compliance by enforcing real-time security policies, detecting access anomalies, and generating compliance reports that document insider threat mitigation efforts. Secure authentication mechanisms, such as MFA and biometric verification, further strengthen IAM security by ensuring that only authorized users can access critical systems.

Privileged access monitoring is a key compliance requirement for mitigating insider threats, as administrative users have extensive control over IT systems. Privileged insiders can exploit elevated permissions to modify system configurations, access confidential data, or disable security controls. PAM solutions enforce just-in-time (JIT) access provisioning, ensuring that privileged users receive temporary permissions only when necessary. IAM compliance frameworks require organizations to log all privileged session activities, enforce real-time monitoring of administrative actions, and integrate PAM with SIEM solutions to detect insider threats in real time. Automated privilege escalation alerts ensure that unauthorized privilege modifications are flagged and investigated immediately.

Third-party access governance is essential for mitigating insider threats posed by external contractors, vendors, and business partners. Organizations frequently grant third-party users temporary access to internal systems, increasing the risk of insider attacks. IAM solutions enforce strict third-party authentication policies, ensuring that external users undergo identity verification before accessing corporate resources. Time-limited access policies ensure that third-party credentials automatically expire after project completion, preventing unauthorized access after engagement termination. Compliance frameworks mandate continuous monitoring of third-party access logs, ensuring that suspicious activities are detected and addressed.

IAM audit processes play a crucial role in insider threat detection and compliance verification. Organizations must implement continuous auditing mechanisms that track access control violations, privilege modifications, and authentication anomalies. IAM solutions generate compliance reports that summarize insider threat incidents, access certification findings, and security policy enforcement actions. Automated IAM audit tools reduce the complexity of compliance reporting, ensuring that organizations can provide regulators with real-time evidence of access governance. By integrating IAM auditing with SIEM solutions, organizations gain visibility into insider threat activities, enabling rapid response to security incidents.

IAM security awareness and training programs ensure that employees, administrators, and third-party users understand the risks associated with insider threats. Organizations must educate users on access control best practices, security policy enforcement, and compliance responsibilities. IAM solutions integrate security training with authentication workflows, requiring users to acknowledge compliance policies, complete periodic security assessments, and follow best practices for access governance. Strengthening security awareness reduces the risk of insider threats by ensuring that employees recognize and report suspicious activities.

Handling insider threats requires organizations to implement comprehensive IAM compliance measures, including least privilege enforcement, privileged access monitoring, continuous authentication, and real-time anomaly detection. By integrating IAM automation, PAM controls, third-party identity governance, and continuous auditing, organizations can detect and mitigate insider threats while ensuring compliance with SOX, GDPR, HIPAA, NIST, and ISO 27001 regulatory frameworks. Implementing IAM compliance measures strengthens identity security, prevents unauthorized access, and ensures that organizations maintain audit-ready access governance policies.

IAM Compliance During Mergers and Acquisitions

Mergers and acquisitions (M&A) present significant challenges for Identity and Access Management (IAM) compliance as organizations integrate users, systems, applications, and data from multiple entities. Regulatory frameworks such as SOX, GDPR, HIPAA, NIST, and ISO 27001 require strict IAM controls to prevent unauthorized access, protect sensitive data, and ensure that identity governance policies remain effective throughout the transition. Failure to enforce IAM compliance during M&A activities can lead to security vulnerabilities, regulatory violations, and operational disruptions. A structured IAM integration strategy ensures that access controls remain consistent, identity risks are mitigated, and compliance obligations are met as organizations merge their IT environments.

IAM due diligence is a critical step in the M&A process, requiring organizations to assess the security posture, identity governance frameworks, and access control policies of the entities involved. Conducting an IAM audit before integration helps identify security gaps, orphan accounts, excessive permissions, and compliance risks associated with identity management practices. Organizations must evaluate the IAM systems used by both parties, determining whether they align with compliance requirements and security best practices. Automated IAM assessment tools analyze access control configurations, privilege assignments, and authentication mechanisms to detect potential compliance violations before system integration begins.

SOX compliance mandates that organizations maintain strict access controls for financial systems, ensuring that only authorized users can modify financial records. During M&A activities, organizations must ensure that IAM policies governing financial data access remain consistent across merged entities. User roles, privilege levels, and authentication methods must be aligned to prevent unauthorized access to financial systems. IAM solutions enforce SOX compliance by generating audit logs that document changes to financial access permissions, tracking privilege escalations, and ensuring that separation of duties (SoD) policies remain intact. Continuous monitoring of financial IAM controls prevents compliance violations and unauthorized transactions during the M&A transition.

The General Data Protection Regulation (GDPR) requires organizations to implement strict data protection measures when processing personal data. IAM compliance during M&A activities ensures that identity governance policies protect personally identifiable information (PII) throughout system integrations. Organizations must evaluate access control policies to ensure that customer data is not exposed to unauthorized personnel during migration processes. IAM solutions enforce GDPR compliance by applying role-based access control (RBAC), enforcing data minimization principles, and generating audit trails that track identity-related access requests. Implementing strict authentication policies, such as multi-factor authentication (MFA), ensures that only authorized personnel access sensitive customer information.

HIPAA mandates that healthcare organizations protect electronic protected health information (ePHI) when consolidating IT systems during mergers and acquisitions. IAM compliance ensures that patient records remain secure as organizations integrate medical applications, databases, and user directories. Healthcare providers must enforce access control policies that prevent unauthorized access to ePHI, ensuring that identity governance frameworks align with HIPAA security rules. IAM automation streamlines HIPAA compliance by continuously monitoring access permissions, generating real-time alerts for suspicious activity, and enforcing privileged access management (PAM) controls to prevent insider threats. Organizations must also conduct IAM security assessments to ensure that legacy access rights from the acquired entity do not violate HIPAA compliance requirements.

NIST guidelines emphasize the importance of risk-based IAM controls during system integrations. Organizations merging IT environments must assess authentication mechanisms, authorization policies, and privilege escalation risks to prevent security vulnerabilities. NIST-compliant IAM frameworks implement continuous monitoring, identity risk scoring, and automated policy enforcement to ensure secure user transitions. Implementing Zero Trust security models ensures that all access requests undergo strict verification before granting user privileges in newly merged IT environments. IAM solutions integrating with behavioral analytics tools help detect anomalous login attempts, preventing credential-based attacks during the transition phase.

ISO 27001 compliance requires organizations to enforce IAM policies that protect information security assets throughout the M&A process. Access control frameworks must be aligned across both entities, ensuring that sensitive data, administrative privileges, and user credentials remain secure. ISO 27001 mandates that organizations establish IAM policies that define how user roles are merged, how authentication systems are integrated, and how access rights are audited post-merger. Automated IAM governance solutions provide visibility into user entitlements, enforcing access reviews that align with ISO 27001 risk management principles. Implementing federated identity management ensures that users from both entities can securely access shared resources without security gaps.

Privileged access management (PAM) plays a crucial role in IAM compliance during M&A activities, as administrative users from both organizations must be integrated into a unified security framework. Privileged accounts have elevated permissions that pose security risks if not managed correctly. Organizations must enforce just-in-time (JIT) access provisioning to grant administrative privileges only when necessary, preventing excessive permissions during the transition. PAM solutions generate session logs, track privileged account activities, and enforce policy-based privilege escalations to mitigate security risks. Organizations must also revoke legacy privileged access permissions that are no longer required post-merger, ensuring that administrative users do not retain unnecessary privileges.

Third-party access governance is another critical compliance concern during M&A activities, as organizations must assess vendor IAM policies to prevent security risks. Merging entities often have separate third-party access frameworks that may not align with compliance requirements. IAM compliance ensures that third-party vendors, contractors, and external users follow standardized authentication policies, ensuring that access rights are granted based on business justifications. Automated IAM solutions monitor third-party access logs, enforce expiration policies for vendor credentials, and generate compliance reports that track external user activities. Enforcing consistent third-party authentication policies prevents security gaps during system integrations.

IAM audit processes ensure that compliance requirements are met throughout the M&A transition. Organizations must conduct periodic IAM reviews that assess access control effectiveness, identify excessive privileges, and enforce security policies. Compliance audits require organizations to provide regulators with access certification reports, demonstrating that identity governance policies remain effective post-merger. IAM automation streamlines compliance reporting by generating real-time dashboards that track authentication trends, access modifications, and identity-related policy violations. Continuous IAM monitoring ensures that security teams detect and remediate access control issues before they result in compliance violations.

IAM security awareness training is essential for ensuring that employees from both merging entities understand new access control policies and compliance obligations. Organizations must conduct IAM training sessions that educate users on authentication requirements, data access policies, and privileged access best practices. IAM solutions integrate compliance training with authentication workflows, ensuring that users acknowledge security policies before accessing critical systems. Strengthening IAM awareness reduces human errors, prevents insider threats, and ensures that employees follow access governance best practices throughout the M&A process.

IAM compliance during mergers and acquisitions requires a structured approach to identity governance, privileged access management, third-party authentication, and continuous monitoring. By enforcing automated IAM controls, conducting security assessments, and aligning access policies across merging entities, organizations can ensure compliance with SOX, GDPR, HIPAA, NIST, and ISO 27001 regulatory requirements. Implementing IAM best practices strengthens security, reduces access control risks, and ensures that identity governance remains effective as organizations transition to a unified IT environment.

IAM Compliance Considerations for Remote Workforces

The shift toward remote work has introduced new challenges for Identity and Access Management (IAM) compliance, requiring organizations to implement robust security measures to protect sensitive data, enforce authentication policies, and maintain regulatory adherence. Regulatory frameworks such as SOX, GDPR, HIPAA, NIST, and ISO 27001 mandate that organizations enforce strict IAM controls to ensure that remote employees, contractors, and third-party users securely access corporate systems. Remote work environments increase the risk of credential-based attacks, unauthorized access, and data breaches, making IAM compliance a critical component of secure remote workforce management.

IAM compliance for remote workforces requires organizations to enforce strong authentication policies that prevent unauthorized access to corporate resources. Multi-factor authentication (MFA) is a fundamental security control that ensures users verify their identity using multiple authentication factors before gaining access to sensitive systems. Regulatory frameworks mandate MFA for remote access, ensuring that employees logging in from external networks undergo strict identity verification. IAM solutions integrate MFA with risk-based authentication (RBA), adjusting authentication requirements based on contextual factors such as login location, device trust level, and access history. Enforcing MFA across remote work environments reduces the risk of credential theft and unauthorized access attempts.

SOX compliance requires organizations to implement strict IAM policies that control access to financial records and reporting systems. Remote employees accessing financial applications must authenticate securely, ensuring that unauthorized users cannot modify financial data. IAM compliance measures include enforcing session timeouts, monitoring login attempts, and tracking authentication logs to detect suspicious activity. Organizations must implement continuous monitoring solutions that analyze remote access patterns, ensuring that security teams receive real-time alerts for policy violations. IAM automation enforces SOX compliance by generating access certification reports, documenting remote user authentication events, and preventing privilege escalations that could compromise financial integrity.

The General Data Protection Regulation (GDPR) mandates strict data protection controls for remote employees handling personally identifiable information (PII). Organizations must enforce IAM policies that restrict access to customer data based on job roles, ensuring that remote users do not retain excessive permissions. IAM solutions enforce data minimization principles by applying least privilege access policies, ensuring that employees only access the information necessary for their job functions. GDPR compliance also requires organizations to encrypt remote authentication sessions, preventing data interception on unsecured networks. IAM monitoring solutions track remote user interactions with PII, ensuring that unauthorized access attempts are detected and mitigated in real time.

HIPAA compliance requires healthcare organizations to implement IAM security controls that protect electronic protected health information (ePHI) accessed by remote employees. Healthcare providers must enforce secure authentication policies that prevent unauthorized access to patient records, ensuring that medical professionals, administrative staff, and IT personnel comply with HIPAA security requirements. IAM automation enforces role-based access control (RBAC), ensuring that remote healthcare workers only access ePHI based on predefined job functions. Privileged access management (PAM) solutions prevent remote administrative users from retaining excessive permissions, enforcing just-in-time (JIT) access provisioning for critical healthcare systems. Continuous IAM monitoring ensures that remote ePHI access remains compliant with HIPAA security standards.

NIST guidelines emphasize the importance of secure remote authentication, identity verification, and continuous access monitoring. Organizations implementing NIST-compliant IAM policies must enforce risk-based authentication, ensuring that remote employees undergo additional verification steps when accessing high-risk systems. Behavioral analytics integrated with IAM solutions detect deviations from normal access patterns, flagging remote login attempts from untrusted devices or locations. Organizations must implement Zero Trust security models, requiring continuous authentication for remote access sessions. IAM compliance automation streamlines NIST compliance by enforcing secure authentication protocols, tracking remote login attempts, and generating audit logs that document access policy enforcement.

ISO 27001 mandates that organizations implement IAM policies that ensure secure remote workforce authentication and access control. Organizations must enforce identity governance frameworks that define how remote employees access corporate systems, ensuring that access rights are assigned, reviewed, and revoked based on compliance requirements. IAM automation enhances ISO 27001 compliance by implementing access certification workflows, ensuring that remote employee permissions are periodically reviewed and adjusted. Session monitoring and remote access logging ensure that organizations maintain audit-ready IAM reports, documenting all authentication attempts, privilege modifications, and security incidents related to remote work environments.

Privileged access management (PAM) plays a critical role in IAM compliance for remote workforces, ensuring that administrative users do not retain excessive privileges beyond necessary job functions. Remote IT administrators, security engineers, and cloud service managers often require privileged access to maintain corporate infrastructure. PAM solutions enforce least privilege policies by granting remote privileged users time-limited access, automatically revoking permissions after task completion. Compliance frameworks require organizations to track privileged session activities, ensuring that remote administrative actions are logged, reviewed, and audited. IAM automation enforces PAM policies by applying just-in-time access provisioning, reducing the risk of privilege abuse in remote work environments.

Third-party remote access governance ensures that external vendors, contractors, and business partners comply with IAM security policies when accessing corporate systems. Compliance frameworks require organizations to enforce strict authentication policies for third-party users, preventing unauthorized access to sensitive data. IAM automation integrates third-party identity governance, enforcing time-restricted access policies and monitoring external user authentication logs. Organizations must implement federated identity management solutions that enable secure third-party authentication while ensuring that external users comply with corporate IAM policies. Continuous monitoring of third-party remote access prevents security breaches and ensures regulatory compliance.

IAM compliance audits ensure that remote workforce security policies align with regulatory requirements, providing organizations with visibility into authentication trends, access violations, and policy enforcement. Organizations must generate IAM audit reports that track remote login attempts, failed authentication events, and privilege modifications. Compliance frameworks require organizations to maintain authentication logs, ensuring that security teams can investigate unauthorized access attempts and enforce remediation actions. IAM automation simplifies compliance auditing by generating real-time dashboards that document remote workforce access trends, policy violations, and security control effectiveness.

IAM training and security awareness programs support compliance enforcement for remote workforces, ensuring that employees understand secure authentication policies, access governance responsibilities, and regulatory obligations. Organizations must conduct remote security training sessions that educate employees on phishing risks, credential hygiene, and compliance best practices. IAM solutions integrate security awareness training with authentication workflows, requiring users to acknowledge access policies, complete periodic compliance assessments, and follow secure remote access protocols. Strengthening IAM awareness among remote employees reduces security risks, preventing compliance violations and identity-related threats.

IAM compliance considerations for remote workforces require organizations to implement strong authentication policies, enforce privileged access management, monitor remote login attempts, and conduct continuous compliance audits. By integrating IAM automation, Zero Trust security models, and third-party identity governance, organizations can secure remote access environments while ensuring compliance with SOX, GDPR, HIPAA, NIST, and ISO 27001 regulatory requirements. Implementing IAM security best practices strengthens identity protection, prevents unauthorized access, and ensures that remote workforce security policies remain aligned with compliance mandates.

Incident Response and IAM Audit Considerations

Incident response and IAM audits are critical components of security and compliance frameworks, ensuring that organizations can detect, investigate, and remediate identity-related security incidents while maintaining regulatory adherence. Identity and Access Management (IAM) plays a fundamental role in incident response by providing visibility into authentication events, user activities, privilege escalations, and unauthorized access attempts. Regulatory standards such as SOX, GDPR, HIPAA, NIST, and ISO 27001 require organizations to implement incident response plans and conduct IAM audits to prevent security breaches, mitigate risks, and maintain compliance with data protection requirements. By integrating IAM with incident response frameworks and audit mechanisms, organizations can ensure that identity-related threats are addressed proactively and access control policies remain enforceable.

IAM-driven incident response begins with real-time monitoring and threat detection, ensuring that organizations can identify security incidents as they occur. Unauthorized access attempts, failed login events, privilege escalations, and abnormal authentication patterns are early indicators of identity-related security breaches. IAM solutions integrated with Security Information and Event Management (SIEM) systems enable organizations to detect suspicious user behavior, enforce automated threat containment, and trigger incident response workflows. Security teams must establish identity-specific response procedures that define how to handle compromised credentials, excessive permissions, and unauthorized privilege escalations. Real-time IAM logging ensures that all authentication attempts, access modifications, and session activities are recorded, providing security teams with actionable intelligence to investigate incidents efficiently.

SOX compliance mandates strict access control and audit requirements to prevent unauthorized modifications to financial systems. IAM audit logs play a critical role in incident response by tracking user access to financial records, detecting unauthorized privilege changes, and generating reports for forensic analysis. Organizations must implement IAM compliance controls that ensure financial system access is continuously monitored and reviewed. IAM automation streamlines SOX compliance by generating audit trails that document access violations, security policy enforcement, and remediation actions taken to mitigate financial fraud risks. Incident response teams must have predefined escalation procedures to investigate IAM policy violations that impact financial data integrity.

The General Data Protection Regulation (GDPR) enforces strict breach notification requirements, mandating that organizations report security incidents involving personally identifiable information (PII) within specific timeframes. IAM incident response ensures that organizations can detect unauthorized access to customer data, assess the scope of the breach, and implement containment measures. IAM audit logs provide security teams with evidence of how PII was accessed, who attempted to retrieve it, and whether compliance policies were violated. IAM-driven forensic investigations enable organizations to demonstrate GDPR compliance by documenting identity-related security incidents, corrective actions taken, and preventive measures implemented to reduce future risks. Continuous monitoring of IAM logs ensures that unauthorized access attempts are detected before customer data is compromised.

HIPAA mandates strict incident response requirements to protect electronic protected health information (ePHI) from unauthorized access, modification, or disclosure. Healthcare organizations must implement IAM policies that enforce access monitoring, privileged account management, and incident response automation to prevent security breaches. IAM audit logs help healthcare providers track access attempts to ePHI, ensuring that unauthorized activities are identified and mitigated. HIPAA compliance requires security teams to document IAM security incidents, enforce risk-based authentication for sensitive healthcare systems, and implement forensic analysis tools to assess identity-related security breaches. IAM-driven incident response ensures that healthcare organizations maintain compliance with HIPAA security rules while protecting patient confidentiality.

NIST guidelines emphasize the importance of incident response automation, continuous monitoring, and forensic investigation capabilities for IAM security. Organizations implementing NIST-compliant IAM policies must ensure that identity-related security incidents are detected, documented, and remediated using structured incident response workflows. IAM automation enhances NIST compliance by integrating with SIEM solutions to detect anomalous authentication events, enforce least privilege access, and generate compliance reports. Incident response teams must establish predefined IAM incident categories, ensuring that unauthorized access attempts, credential compromise incidents, and privilege escalation attacks are handled efficiently. IAM audit considerations include tracking failed login events, monitoring high-risk user activities, and enforcing multi-factor authentication (MFA) for security-sensitive operations.

ISO 27001 mandates that organizations implement an Information Security Management System (ISMS) that includes IAM-driven incident response procedures and audit policies. Organizations must define access control policies that regulate how security incidents involving user identities are handled, ensuring that unauthorized access attempts are detected and mitigated. IAM compliance controls for ISO 27001 include real-time authentication monitoring, automated incident escalation, and access review enforcement. IAM audit logs provide security teams with insights into access control policy violations, privilege modifications, and security incidents affecting user identities. Organizations must conduct periodic IAM audits to assess identity governance effectiveness, ensuring that security policies align with ISO 27001 compliance requirements.

Privileged access management (PAM) plays a crucial role in IAM incident response by ensuring that privileged accounts are continuously monitored, controlled, and audited. Privileged accounts have elevated permissions that, if compromised, can lead to data breaches, unauthorized system modifications, and compliance violations. IAM automation enhances privileged access security by enforcing just-in-time (JIT) access provisioning, session recording, and anomaly detection for privileged account activities. Incident response teams must implement IAM audit procedures that review privileged session logs, detect unauthorized privilege escalations, and enforce real-time remediation measures to contain security risks. Compliance frameworks require organizations to generate privileged access audit reports that document security incidents, corrective actions, and policy adjustments.

Third-party IAM security incidents pose additional compliance challenges, as organizations frequently grant external vendors, contractors, and business partners access to internal systems. IAM incident response ensures that third-party authentication attempts, access requests, and identity-related security events are continuously monitored and reviewed. Regulatory frameworks require organizations to implement third-party identity governance policies that enforce access control restrictions, time-limited authentication sessions, and automated account deactivation for inactive external users. IAM audit considerations for third-party access include tracking authentication failures, monitoring remote login attempts, and enforcing compliance assessments to verify that third-party identity risks are mitigated.

IAM audit processes enhance incident response capabilities by ensuring that security teams have visibility into authentication patterns, access anomalies, and compliance violations. Organizations must conduct periodic IAM audits that assess access governance effectiveness, track security policy enforcement, and detect unauthorized identity-related activities. IAM automation generates compliance reports that document audit findings, identity risk assessments, and incident response measures. Security teams must ensure that IAM audit logs are securely stored, encrypted, and analyzed to detect emerging security threats. IAM compliance audits provide regulators with evidence of identity governance effectiveness, ensuring that organizations meet regulatory standards for incident response and security monitoring.

IAM security awareness training ensures that employees, administrators, and security teams understand incident response best practices and compliance obligations. Organizations must conduct security training programs that educate users on identity threat detection, secure authentication practices, and access governance policies. IAM solutions integrate security awareness training with incident response workflows, requiring employees to acknowledge security policies, complete compliance assessments, and follow identity security best practices. Strengthening IAM security awareness ensures that employees recognize identity-related threats, report suspicious authentication attempts, and comply with incident response policies.

Incident response and IAM audit considerations are essential for maintaining compliance with SOX, GDPR, HIPAA, NIST, and ISO 27001 regulatory requirements. By implementing automated IAM monitoring, privileged access governance, third-party identity risk management, and continuous security assessments, organizations can detect identity-related threats, enforce access control policies, and ensure regulatory compliance. IAM-driven incident response strengthens security resilience, reduces identity fraud risks, and ensures that organizations maintain audit-ready access governance frameworks.

Conducting IAM Gap Assessments for Compliance

Identity and Access Management (IAM) gap assessments are critical for organizations seeking to maintain compliance with regulatory frameworks such as SOX, GDPR, HIPAA, NIST, and ISO 27001. A gap assessment evaluates the current state of IAM controls, policies, and enforcement mechanisms to identify security deficiencies, access control weaknesses, and compliance risks. Organizations must regularly conduct IAM gap assessments to ensure that identity governance remains effective, access management policies align with compliance mandates, and identity-related security threats are addressed proactively. By identifying gaps in IAM controls, organizations can implement remediation measures, enhance security posture, and maintain regulatory compliance.

The first step in conducting an IAM gap assessment is defining the scope of the evaluation, ensuring that all identity-related components, including user authentication, access control policies, privileged account management, and third-party identity governance, are reviewed. Organizations must assess IAM policies across on-premises systems, cloud environments, and hybrid IT infrastructures to ensure that access control consistency is maintained. Compliance frameworks mandate that organizations document IAM policies, define identity governance roles, and enforce access control mechanisms that prevent unauthorized access to sensitive systems and data. A structured IAM gap assessment provides visibility into compliance weaknesses, ensuring that corrective actions are implemented.

SOX compliance requires organizations to implement IAM controls that protect financial records, enforce strict authentication policies, and prevent unauthorized privilege escalations. IAM gap assessments for SOX compliance focus on evaluating role-based access controls (RBAC), multi-factor authentication (MFA) enforcement, and privileged account security. Organizations must assess whether financial system access permissions are properly assigned, ensuring that employees do not retain excessive privileges that could be exploited for fraudulent activities. IAM automation enhances SOX compliance by identifying policy deviations, generating access certification reports, and enforcing corrective measures to remediate identity-related security gaps.

The General Data Protection Regulation (GDPR) enforces strict data protection requirements, mandating that organizations prevent unauthorized access to personally identifiable information (PII). IAM gap assessments for GDPR compliance evaluate access governance policies, user authentication mechanisms, and identity monitoring practices to ensure that PII remains protected. Organizations must assess data minimization principles, ensuring that users only access PII necessary for their job functions. IAM gap assessments detect excessive permissions, orphaned accounts, and authentication weaknesses that could lead to non-compliance penalties. By integrating IAM automation, organizations enforce real-time identity verification, access monitoring, and compliance reporting to ensure GDPR adherence.

HIPAA compliance mandates that healthcare organizations protect electronic protected health information (ePHI) through IAM controls that restrict access to patient records, enforce authentication policies, and monitor identity-related security events. IAM gap assessments for HIPAA compliance focus on evaluating user authentication mechanisms, privileged access management (PAM) enforcement, and third-party identity governance. Healthcare organizations must assess whether administrative, clinical, and IT personnel have appropriate access levels, ensuring that excessive permissions do not expose ePHI to unauthorized users. IAM automation supports HIPAA compliance by detecting unauthorized access attempts, enforcing real-time security alerts, and ensuring that all identity-related activities are logged for compliance audits.

NIST guidelines emphasize risk-based IAM controls, continuous authentication monitoring, and zero trust security enforcement. IAM gap assessments for NIST compliance evaluate identity risk scoring mechanisms, access anomaly detection capabilities, and IAM integration with Security Information and Event Management (SIEM) solutions. Organizations must assess IAM automation policies that enforce dynamic authentication requirements based on user behavior, login patterns, and contextual risk factors. IAM gap assessments detect weaknesses in authentication policies, privilege escalation risks, and inconsistent enforcement of least privilege access controls. Implementing IAM automation ensures that organizations maintain NIST compliance by enforcing continuous access monitoring and identity threat detection.

ISO 27001 mandates that organizations establish IAM security policies that regulate user access, enforce privileged account monitoring, and prevent unauthorized data exposure. IAM gap assessments for ISO 27001 compliance evaluate access control frameworks, authentication enforcement policies, and identity governance procedures. Organizations must assess whether IAM policies align with ISO 27001 risk management principles, ensuring that access control weaknesses are remediated. IAM automation enhances ISO 27001 compliance by generating access review reports, tracking authentication logs, and enforcing security policies that prevent unauthorized system access. IAM gap assessments provide organizations with insights into compliance gaps, ensuring that corrective actions are implemented to strengthen IAM security.

Privileged access management (PAM) plays a critical role in IAM gap assessments, ensuring that privileged accounts are protected from unauthorized access and privilege abuse. Organizations must assess whether privileged users have excessive permissions, whether privileged session activities are logged, and whether privileged access policies are enforced. IAM automation enhances PAM security by enforcing just-in-time (JIT) privileged access provisioning, ensuring that administrative permissions are granted only when necessary and revoked after task completion. IAM gap assessments detect weaknesses in privileged access controls, ensuring that privileged user activities remain compliant with regulatory requirements.

Third-party identity governance is another critical compliance concern evaluated during IAM gap assessments, as organizations frequently grant vendors, contractors, and external users access to internal systems. Organizations must assess whether third-party authentication policies, access approval workflows, and monitoring controls align with compliance requirements. IAM automation ensures that third-party credentials are time-restricted, continuously monitored, and automatically deactivated when access is no longer needed. IAM gap assessments detect risks associated with external identity governance, ensuring that third-party authentication practices remain secure and compliant.

IAM audit processes play a crucial role in gap assessments, providing organizations with visibility into authentication patterns, privilege modifications, and access violations. Organizations must conduct periodic IAM gap assessments to evaluate access governance effectiveness, ensuring that identity-related security policies remain enforceable. IAM automation generates compliance reports that summarize IAM policy gaps, security risk assessments, and remediation actions. IAM audit considerations include tracking orphan accounts, monitoring failed authentication attempts, and ensuring that privileged access violations are identified and mitigated. By continuously assessing IAM policies, organizations can maintain compliance with regulatory mandates while preventing identity-related security breaches.

IAM security awareness training supports gap assessment initiatives by educating employees, administrators, and security teams on compliance responsibilities and identity security best practices. Organizations must conduct IAM security training sessions that reinforce authentication best practices, access policy enforcement, and compliance obligations. IAM solutions integrate security awareness training with access management policies, requiring users to acknowledge security policies, complete compliance assessments, and follow least privilege access principles. Strengthening IAM awareness ensures that employees recognize security risks, adhere to identity governance policies, and follow best practices for compliance enforcement.

Conducting IAM gap assessments for compliance ensures that organizations identify identity security weaknesses, remediate access control deficiencies, and maintain adherence to SOX, GDPR, HIPAA, NIST, and ISO 27001 regulatory requirements. By integrating IAM automation, privileged access management, third-party identity governance, and continuous security monitoring, organizations can enforce access control policies, detect security violations, and ensure that IAM policies remain effective. Regular IAM gap assessments strengthen identity governance, prevent unauthorized access, and enhance compliance enforcement across IT environments.

IAM Risk Management Frameworks and Methodologies

Identity and Access Management (IAM) risk management frameworks and methodologies are essential for organizations to mitigate security threats, prevent unauthorized access, and ensure compliance with regulatory mandates. IAM risk management involves identifying, assessing, and mitigating risks associated with user authentication, access provisioning, privilege escalation, and identity governance. Regulatory frameworks such as SOX, GDPR, HIPAA, NIST, and ISO 27001 mandate that organizations implement structured IAM risk management strategies to protect sensitive data and enforce access control policies. By leveraging IAM risk management frameworks, organizations can proactively address identity-related security risks, enforce least privilege access, and strengthen IAM governance.

IAM risk management begins with risk identification, ensuring that organizations can detect access control weaknesses, authentication vulnerabilities, and privilege escalation risks. Organizations must assess IAM policies across on-premises systems, cloud environments, and hybrid IT infrastructures to identify security gaps. Risk assessment methodologies such as threat modeling, risk scoring, and attack surface analysis provide organizations with insights into identity-related security threats. Automated IAM risk assessment tools analyze authentication logs, access patterns, and privilege assignment configurations to detect anomalies and policy violations. By conducting IAM risk identification processes, organizations gain visibility into security vulnerabilities and compliance risks associated with identity governance.

SOX compliance requires organizations to enforce IAM risk management strategies that prevent unauthorized modifications to financial records. IAM risk assessment methodologies for SOX compliance focus on evaluating authentication policies, privilege escalation risks, and access review enforcement. Organizations must implement IAM risk management frameworks that enforce multi-factor authentication (MFA), privileged access monitoring, and continuous access logging for financial systems. IAM automation enhances SOX risk management by detecting unauthorized financial access attempts, enforcing least privilege policies, and generating risk assessment reports that document IAM security weaknesses.

The General Data Protection Regulation (GDPR) mandates that organizations implement IAM risk management methodologies that protect personally identifiable information (PII) from unauthorized access. IAM risk assessments for GDPR compliance focus on evaluating access governance policies, data protection measures, and identity monitoring controls. Organizations must assess identity risk factors, ensuring that user permissions align with business requirements and that excessive privileges do not expose customer data. IAM automation enforces GDPR risk management by implementing access certification workflows, detecting unauthorized data access attempts, and enforcing real-time authentication monitoring. IAM risk mitigation strategies ensure that organizations maintain compliance with GDPR data protection mandates.

HIPAA compliance requires healthcare organizations to implement IAM risk management frameworks that prevent unauthorized access to electronic protected health information (ePHI). IAM risk assessments for HIPAA compliance evaluate authentication mechanisms, access control policies, and privileged account security. Healthcare organizations must enforce IAM risk management methodologies that detect security anomalies, monitor access to patient records, and prevent privilege abuse. IAM automation enhances HIPAA risk management by continuously monitoring ePHI access attempts, detecting suspicious login patterns, and generating compliance reports that track IAM security risks. Enforcing IAM risk mitigation measures ensures that healthcare organizations protect patient data and maintain HIPAA compliance.

NIST guidelines emphasize risk-based IAM security controls, requiring organizations to implement IAM risk assessment frameworks that detect authentication vulnerabilities and privilege escalation risks.

IAM risk management methodologies for NIST compliance involve continuous monitoring, adaptive authentication, and behavioral risk analysis. Organizations must assess IAM security risks based on user behavior, session activity, and contextual factors such as device trust levels and geographic locations. IAM automation enhances NIST risk management by integrating machine learning-based risk scoring models, detecting access anomalies, and enforcing policy-based security controls. Implementing IAM risk management methodologies ensures that organizations maintain compliance with NIST cybersecurity standards.

ISO 27001 mandates that organizations implement an Information Security Management System (ISMS) that includes IAM risk management policies. IAM risk assessment methodologies for ISO 27001 compliance evaluate access control effectiveness, privileged session monitoring, and identity governance enforcement. Organizations must implement IAM risk mitigation frameworks that prevent unauthorized access, enforce access review processes, and detect privilege escalation threats. IAM automation enhances ISO 27001 risk management by generating security reports that document access policy violations, implementing automated access revocation mechanisms, and ensuring that identity-related security incidents are addressed proactively.

Privileged access risk management is a critical component of IAM security, ensuring that privileged accounts do not become targets for insider threats or external attacks. IAM risk management frameworks enforce privileged access monitoring, session recording, and just-in-time (JIT) privileged access provisioning to mitigate security risks. Organizations must assess privileged access risk factors, ensuring that administrative users do not retain excessive permissions that could be exploited for malicious purposes. IAM automation enhances privileged access risk management by detecting unauthorized privilege escalations, enforcing access expiration policies, and integrating with Security Information and Event Management (SIEM) solutions for real-time threat detection.

Third-party identity risk management ensures that external vendors, contractors, and business partners do not introduce security vulnerabilities into corporate IAM environments. Organizations must assess third-party IAM risk factors, ensuring that external users comply with authentication policies, access control enforcement, and compliance mandates. IAM risk management frameworks enforce third-party identity verification, ensuring that vendors undergo strict authentication before accessing corporate systems. IAM automation enhances third-party risk management by enforcing time-limited access policies, tracking third-party authentication logs, and detecting unauthorized third-party access attempts. Implementing IAM risk mitigation measures reduces supply chain security risks and ensures regulatory compliance.

IAM audit processes play a crucial role in risk management, providing organizations with visibility into authentication failures, privilege violations, and access control policy deviations. Organizations must conduct periodic IAM risk assessments that evaluate security weaknesses, enforce access certification, and detect insider threats. IAM automation enhances risk management auditing by generating compliance reports that document IAM policy violations, tracking security incident trends, and enforcing automated remediation workflows. Continuous IAM risk monitoring ensures that organizations maintain compliance with regulatory mandates while preventing identity-related security incidents.

IAM security awareness training supports risk management initiatives by educating employees, administrators, and security teams on identity security risks, authentication policies, and compliance obligations. Organizations must implement IAM training programs that reinforce secure authentication practices, privileged access management best practices, and insider threat detection strategies. IAM automation integrates security training with authentication workflows, requiring users to acknowledge compliance policies, complete periodic risk awareness assessments, and follow identity governance best practices. Strengthening IAM security awareness ensures that employees recognize identity-related security threats, adhere to access control policies, and follow IAM risk mitigation strategies.

IAM risk management frameworks and methodologies provide organizations with structured approaches to identifying, assessing, and mitigating identity-related security risks. By integrating IAM automation, privileged access risk management, third-party identity governance, and continuous security monitoring, organizations can enforce IAM security policies, detect authentication anomalies, and ensure compliance with SOX, GDPR, HIPAA, NIST, and ISO 27001 regulatory requirements. Implementing IAM risk management best practices enhances identity governance, reduces security vulnerabilities, and ensures that IAM policies remain enforceable across IT environments.

IAM Compliance Testing and Validation Techniques

IAM compliance testing and validation techniques are essential for ensuring that identity and access management controls align with regulatory frameworks such as SOX, GDPR, HIPAA, NIST, and ISO 27001. Organizations must conduct regular testing to verify that authentication policies, access controls, and privilege management measures function as intended to prevent unauthorized access, detect security gaps, and maintain regulatory adherence. By implementing structured IAM compliance testing methodologies, organizations can identify policy deviations, enforce corrective actions, and strengthen identity governance. Automated IAM validation techniques enhance security monitoring, detect authentication anomalies, and ensure continuous compliance enforcement.

IAM compliance testing begins with access control verification, ensuring that user roles, permissions, and authentication mechanisms align with security policies. Organizations must validate role-based access control (RBAC) and attribute-based access control (ABAC) configurations, ensuring that users receive appropriate access privileges based on job functions. Compliance frameworks mandate that access control policies enforce least privilege principles, preventing users from accumulating excessive permissions over time. Automated IAM testing solutions analyze access control configurations, detecting misconfigurations, unauthorized privilege escalations, and orphan accounts. Regular access control testing ensures that IAM policies remain enforceable and that security risks associated with excessive permissions are mitigated.

SOX compliance requires organizations to conduct IAM testing that verifies authentication security, privileged access enforcement, and financial system access controls. IAM validation techniques for SOX compliance include testing multi-factor authentication (MFA) mechanisms, verifying access certification workflows, and conducting privilege escalation audits. Organizations must implement IAM testing procedures that simulate unauthorized access attempts, ensuring that security policies prevent privilege abuse. Automated IAM validation enhances SOX compliance by generating security reports that track authentication failures, access review effectiveness, and policy enforcement. Continuous IAM testing ensures that financial system access remains restricted to authorized personnel, preventing fraudulent activities.

The General Data Protection Regulation (GDPR) mandates that organizations enforce strict IAM security controls to protect personally identifiable information (PII). IAM compliance testing for GDPR validation includes assessing data access policies, validating encryption mechanisms, and enforcing authentication monitoring. Organizations must conduct IAM penetration testing that simulates unauthorized access attempts to detect weaknesses in authentication workflows. Automated IAM compliance validation enforces GDPR testing requirements by monitoring user interactions with PII, tracking access policy violations, and ensuring that identity verification procedures align with data protection mandates. IAM security testing ensures that personal data remains protected from unauthorized exposure and that access governance policies remain enforceable.

HIPAA compliance testing ensures that healthcare organizations implement IAM security controls that prevent unauthorized access to electronic protected health information (ePHI). IAM validation techniques for HIPAA compliance include testing privileged account access, enforcing session monitoring, and validating identity authentication policies. Healthcare organizations must conduct IAM security assessments that verify user role enforcement, ensuring that doctors, nurses, and administrative staff have access only to necessary patient records. Automated IAM testing detects unauthorized ePHI access attempts, enforces real-time compliance alerts, and ensures that access control policies align with HIPAA security mandates. IAM penetration testing evaluates the effectiveness of authentication security, ensuring that ePHI remains protected from unauthorized disclosure.

NIST guidelines emphasize the importance of IAM security testing, requiring organizations to validate authentication mechanisms, risk-based access policies, and identity threat detection capabilities. IAM compliance testing for NIST frameworks includes evaluating continuous authentication enforcement, testing access anomaly detection models, and validating IAM policy enforcement mechanisms. Organizations must conduct IAM vulnerability assessments that identify weaknesses in user identity verification, access request workflows, and privileged account security. Automated IAM validation enhances NIST compliance by integrating security analytics, enforcing adaptive authentication testing, and generating IAM security assessment reports that track compliance enforcement effectiveness.

ISO 27001 mandates that organizations implement IAM compliance testing methodologies that assess access control effectiveness, identity governance enforcement, and privileged access security. IAM validation techniques for ISO 27001 compliance include testing identity lifecycle management processes, verifying authentication logging mechanisms, and enforcing IAM risk assessment models. Organizations must conduct IAM security audits that validate access review policies, ensuring that identity governance measures remain compliant with ISO 27001 security controls. Automated IAM testing solutions generate compliance validation reports that document access policy enforcement, authentication security effectiveness, and identity-related risk assessments. Regular IAM compliance testing ensures that ISO 27001 security mandates remain enforceable across IT environments.

Privileged access testing is a critical component of IAM compliance validation, ensuring that administrative users do not retain excessive privileges that could lead to insider threats or unauthorized system modifications. Organizations must implement IAM security assessments that validate privileged access policies, enforce just-in-time (JIT) access provisioning, and track privileged session activities. Automated IAM compliance testing for privileged access management

(PAM) detects privilege abuse, unauthorized privilege escalations, and policy violations. IAM testing methodologies enforce privileged session recording, ensuring that administrative actions are monitored, logged, and reviewed for compliance auditing. IAM penetration testing evaluates PAM security, ensuring that privileged accounts remain protected from unauthorized exploitation.

Third-party IAM compliance testing ensures that vendor authentication policies, external user access controls, and contractor identity verification procedures align with regulatory requirements. Organizations must conduct IAM security assessments that validate third-party identity governance, ensuring that external users follow strict authentication policies and least privilege access principles. Automated IAM compliance testing enforces time-limited access policies, tracks third-party authentication logs, and detects unauthorized external access attempts. IAM validation techniques for third-party compliance include testing federated identity management workflows, enforcing third-party authentication monitoring, and ensuring that external access privileges expire automatically when no longer required.

IAM audit testing enhances compliance validation by ensuring that authentication policies, access certification workflows, and privileged session controls function as expected. Organizations must conduct periodic IAM audits that validate access review policies, monitor identity policy enforcement, and detect unauthorized access modifications. IAM automation enhances compliance audit validation by generating security reports that track IAM policy deviations, authentication failure trends, and privilege assignment effectiveness. IAM security testing ensures that organizations maintain audit readiness, providing regulators with detailed compliance validation reports that document identity governance effectiveness.

IAM training and security awareness programs support compliance testing by ensuring that employees, security teams, and IT administrators understand IAM security best practices and policy enforcement requirements. Organizations must conduct IAM training sessions that reinforce authentication security principles, access governance responsibilities, and privileged access management enforcement. IAM automation integrates compliance training with security testing workflows, requiring users to acknowledge access policies, complete security assessments, and follow authentication best practices. Strengthening IAM security awareness ensures that users adhere to compliance policies, preventing security violations and enhancing identity risk management.

IAM compliance testing and validation techniques provide organizations with structured approaches to evaluating authentication security, access governance enforcement, and privileged access management controls. By integrating IAM automation, security analytics, and continuous testing methodologies, organizations can detect identity-related security threats, enforce regulatory compliance, and prevent unauthorized access. Implementing IAM compliance testing best practices enhances identity governance, strengthens security posture, and ensures that IAM policies remain effective across IT environments.

Addressing IAM Compliance Violations and Remediation

Identity and Access Management (IAM) compliance violations pose significant security and regulatory risks, requiring organizations to implement structured remediation strategies to mitigate threats, enforce security policies, and maintain regulatory adherence. Compliance frameworks such as SOX, GDPR, HIPAA, NIST, and ISO 27001 mandate that organizations establish IAM enforcement mechanisms that detect, investigate, and correct identity governance violations. Failure to address IAM compliance violations can result in data breaches, unauthorized access, financial fraud, and regulatory penalties. Organizations must implement automated IAM compliance monitoring, continuous auditing, and policy enforcement workflows to ensure that IAM violations are detected and remediated in real time.

IAM compliance violations occur when users gain unauthorized access to systems, accumulate excessive privileges, bypass authentication controls, or fail to adhere to identity governance policies. Organizations must categorize IAM compliance violations based on risk severity, ensuring that high-risk violations, such as unauthorized privileged access, are remediated immediately. Automated IAM compliance enforcement detects policy deviations, generating alerts that notify security teams of access anomalies, authentication failures, and privilege escalation attempts. By implementing IAM compliance dashboards, organizations gain visibility into identity governance weaknesses, ensuring that violations are addressed before they lead to security incidents.

SOX compliance mandates that organizations enforce strict IAM policies that prevent unauthorized modifications to financial records. IAM compliance violations for SOX regulations include unauthorized access to financial data, privilege abuse, and failure to enforce multi-factor authentication (MFA) for financial system access. Organizations must conduct IAM compliance audits that assess user entitlements, ensuring that financial personnel do not retain excessive permissions beyond their job functions. Automated IAM remediation solutions revoke unauthorized access, enforce role-based access control (RBAC) policies, and generate audit reports that document compliance corrections. IAM policy enforcement ensures that financial system security aligns with SOX access control requirements.

The General Data Protection Regulation (GDPR) enforces strict IAM policies that protect personally identifiable information (PII) from unauthorized access and data exposure. IAM compliance violations under GDPR include unauthorized data access attempts, failure to enforce access logging, and excessive privilege retention. Organizations must implement IAM policy enforcement workflows that detect PII access violations, ensuring that security teams receive real-time alerts when identity governance policies are breached. IAM remediation strategies include automated access reviews, immediate privilege revocation for unauthorized data access, and continuous IAM policy validation. Compliance reporting ensures that organizations provide regulators with documented evidence of access control enforcement, ensuring GDPR adherence.

HIPAA compliance requires healthcare organizations to implement IAM security controls that prevent unauthorized access to electronic protected health information (ePHI). IAM compliance violations for HIPAA include unauthorized access to patient records, privilege misuse by medical staff, and failure to enforce authentication controls. Organizations must conduct IAM security assessments that evaluate ePHI access patterns, ensuring that compliance violations are detected before they result in regulatory penalties. IAM automation enforces HIPAA compliance by implementing real-time session monitoring, generating alerts for suspicious ePHI access, and enforcing role-based access restrictions. IAM remediation workflows ensure that unauthorized access attempts trigger immediate privilege revocation and compliance incident reporting.

NIST guidelines emphasize the importance of IAM compliance enforcement, requiring organizations to implement identity threat detection, continuous authentication validation, and real-time access control enforcement. IAM compliance violations under NIST frameworks include unauthorized privilege escalations, access control misconfigurations, and failure to enforce risk-based authentication (RBA). Organizations must implement IAM compliance automation that detects security anomalies, ensuring that IAM violations are remediated through policy-based security enforcement. IAM security intelligence platforms integrate with Security Information and Event Management (SIEM) solutions, detecting IAM compliance deviations and generating automated remediation workflows that enforce access control policies. IAM compliance monitoring ensures that NIST security requirements remain enforceable across IT environments.

ISO 27001 mandates that organizations implement IAM compliance enforcement mechanisms that detect unauthorized access, enforce privileged access management (PAM), and validate authentication security policies. IAM compliance violations for ISO 27001 include orphan account accumulation, excessive administrative privileges, and failure to enforce access certification reviews. Organizations must conduct IAM audits that assess access control effectiveness, ensuring that user authentication policies align with ISO 27001 security mandates. IAM automation enhances ISO 27001 compliance by generating compliance incident reports, tracking privilege modifications, and enforcing policy-based security controls. IAM remediation workflows ensure that access control violations trigger immediate security enforcement measures.

Privileged access violations are among the most critical IAM compliance risks, as privileged accounts grant elevated permissions that can be exploited for unauthorized system modifications. IAM compliance violations for privileged access management (PAM) include excessive privilege retention, unauthorized privilege escalations, and failure to enforce privileged session monitoring. Organizations must implement IAM enforcement mechanisms that detect privileged account misuse, ensuring that excessive permissions are revoked through automated remediation workflows. PAM solutions enforce just-in-time (JIT) privileged access provisioning, ensuring that administrative permissions are granted temporarily and automatically revoked after task completion. IAM security monitoring ensures that privileged access violations trigger compliance incident response workflows.

Third-party IAM compliance enforcement ensures that vendors, contractors, and business partners adhere to strict authentication policies, access control policies, and identity governance regulations. IAM compliance violations for third-party access include unauthorized vendor authentication attempts, failure to enforce time-limited access permissions, and excessive third-party user privileges. Organizations must implement IAM automation that tracks third-party authentication logs, ensuring that unauthorized access attempts trigger immediate security enforcement. IAM remediation workflows enforce access revocation for non-compliant third-party users, ensuring that vendor authentication credentials expire automatically when no longer needed. IAM compliance monitoring ensures that third-party access security remains enforceable.

IAM compliance audits provide organizations with visibility into identity governance policy violations, ensuring that security teams detect authentication failures, privilege misconfigurations, and access policy enforcement weaknesses. Organizations must conduct periodic IAM compliance audits that validate authentication security effectiveness, track access governance policy enforcement, and ensure that identity security measures remain compliant with regulatory mandates. IAM compliance automation enhances audit readiness by generating security reports that track IAM policy deviations, authentication failure trends, and access governance effectiveness. IAM compliance dashboards provide organizations with real-time security insights, ensuring that compliance violations are addressed immediately.

IAM security awareness training ensures that employees, administrators, and third-party users understand compliance policies, authentication best practices, and identity security responsibilities. Organizations must implement IAM training programs that educate users on access control enforcement, compliance policy adherence, and privilege security best practices. IAM automation integrates security training with compliance enforcement workflows, ensuring that users acknowledge IAM policies, complete periodic compliance assessments, and follow authentication security best practices. Strengthening IAM security awareness reduces compliance violations, preventing unauthorized access attempts and privilege escalation threats.

IAM compliance violation detection and remediation require organizations to implement IAM security automation, continuous monitoring, and regulatory enforcement mechanisms. By integrating IAM policy enforcement, privileged access governance, third-party identity governance, and automated remediation workflows, organizations can detect security violations, enforce compliance policies, and maintain adherence to SOX, GDPR, HIPAA, NIST, and ISO 27001 regulatory requirements. Implementing IAM security enforcement best practices strengthens identity governance, reduces security risks, and ensures that IAM compliance violations are addressed before they lead to regulatory penalties.

Audit Preparation for SOX, GDPR, HIPAA, NIST, and ISO 27001

Preparing for audits under regulatory frameworks such as SOX, GDPR, HIPAA, NIST, and ISO 27001 requires organizations to implement structured Identity and Access Management (IAM) compliance measures. Audits assess access control enforcement, identity governance policies, authentication mechanisms, and security monitoring practices to ensure regulatory adherence. Organizations must conduct pre-audit assessments, generate compliance reports, and implement IAM automation to streamline audit readiness. By enforcing security controls, documenting IAM policy enforcement, and maintaining audit trails, organizations can demonstrate compliance with industry standards while mitigating regulatory risks.

IAM audit preparation begins with data collection and documentation, ensuring that authentication logs, privilege assignments, and access control policies align with compliance requirements. Organizations must maintain detailed records of user access requests, privilege modifications, and authentication attempts, ensuring that IAM policies are enforced consistently. Regulatory frameworks mandate that organizations implement continuous monitoring mechanisms that detect access anomalies, privilege escalations, and unauthorized authentication attempts. IAM compliance automation generates audit-ready reports, ensuring that auditors receive comprehensive documentation of identity governance enforcement.

SOX compliance audits focus on IAM security controls that protect financial systems, enforce privileged access monitoring, and prevent unauthorized modifications to financial data. Organizations must implement IAM policies that restrict financial system access to authorized users, ensuring that authentication mechanisms enforce multi-factor authentication (MFA) and least privilege access. SOX audit preparation includes generating IAM access certification reports, tracking financial system login attempts, and enforcing access review workflows. IAM automation enhances SOX audit readiness by detecting unauthorized privilege escalations, enforcing separation of duties (SoD) policies, and generating real-time compliance dashboards that document financial access security measures.

The General Data Protection Regulation (GDPR) mandates that organizations implement IAM policies that protect personally identifiable information (PII) from unauthorized access and data exposure. GDPR audit preparation includes validating access governance policies, enforcing data minimization principles, and ensuring that user authentication logs comply with data retention mandates. Organizations must generate IAM compliance reports that document PII access patterns, authentication enforcement measures, and identity verification policies. IAM automation enforces GDPR compliance by detecting unauthorized data access attempts, tracking access policy violations, and generating real-time compliance audit logs. GDPR audit readiness requires organizations to document IAM policy enforcement measures, ensuring that auditors receive detailed evidence of identity governance effectiveness.

HIPAA compliance audits require healthcare organizations to implement IAM security controls that protect electronic protected health information (ePHI). IAM audit preparation for HIPAA compliance includes enforcing privileged access management (PAM), conducting authentication security assessments, and generating compliance reports that document ePHI access enforcement. Healthcare organizations must validate that medical personnel, administrative staff, and IT administrators adhere to HIPAA authentication policies, ensuring that IAM policies prevent unauthorized ePHI access. IAM automation enhances HIPAA audit readiness by generating security alerts for suspicious ePHI access attempts, enforcing session monitoring for privileged users, and providing compliance reports that document IAM security enforcement.

NIST compliance audits emphasize IAM security enforcement, requiring organizations to implement continuous authentication monitoring, risk-based access controls, and identity threat detection mechanisms. IAM audit preparation for NIST frameworks includes evaluating identity risk assessment models, testing adaptive authentication mechanisms, and enforcing zero trust security principles. Organizations must generate IAM security reports that track user authentication patterns, detect anomalous access attempts, and validate access control effectiveness. IAM automation enhances NIST audit readiness by integrating with Security Information and Event Management (SIEM) solutions, ensuring that IAM compliance violations trigger real-time security enforcement actions.

ISO 27001 mandates that organizations implement IAM security policies that regulate user access, enforce privileged account monitoring, and prevent unauthorized identity modifications. IAM audit preparation for ISO 27001 compliance includes conducting access control effectiveness assessments, validating IAM policy enforcement mechanisms, and ensuring that security monitoring practices remain aligned with compliance mandates. Organizations must generate IAM compliance reports that document privileged account security measures, authentication logging enforcement, and identity governance policy adherence. IAM automation enhances ISO 27001 audit readiness by generating access certification logs, enforcing automated access review workflows, and detecting identity governance policy deviations.

Privileged access audit preparation ensures that administrative users, IT personnel, and security engineers adhere to IAM security controls that prevent privilege abuse. Compliance frameworks mandate that organizations implement PAM security measures that restrict privileged account access, enforce just-in-time (JIT) privileged access provisioning, and track administrative session activities. IAM automation enhances privileged access audit readiness by generating privileged session monitoring reports, enforcing privileged access expiration policies, and detecting unauthorized privilege escalations. Audit preparation for privileged access compliance ensures that IAM policies prevent insider threats, privilege abuse, and unauthorized system modifications.

Third-party IAM audit preparation ensures that external vendors, contractors, and business partners adhere to authentication policies, access control regulations, and identity governance mandates. Organizations must validate third-party authentication mechanisms, ensuring that vendor access requests comply with IAM security policies. IAM automation enhances third-party audit readiness by generating authentication logs for external users, enforcing third-party access expiration policies, and detecting unauthorized vendor access attempts. IAM compliance reporting ensures that auditors receive detailed documentation of third-party identity governance measures, preventing regulatory penalties and security violations.

IAM compliance audit processes provide organizations with visibility into authentication policy enforcement, access control policy effectiveness, and privilege security monitoring. Organizations must conduct periodic IAM audits that assess compliance policy adherence, detect security control weaknesses, and enforce identity governance best practices. IAM automation enhances audit readiness by generating compliance dashboards that track access violations, authentication anomalies, and identity security trends. IAM compliance reports provide auditors with structured evidence of IAM policy enforcement, ensuring that organizations maintain adherence to SOX, GDPR, HIPAA, NIST, and ISO 27001 regulatory mandates.

IAM security awareness training ensures that employees, administrators, and security teams understand compliance responsibilities, authentication best practices, and access control enforcement measures. Organizations must conduct IAM training programs that reinforce identity governance policies, privilege access security requirements, and regulatory compliance mandates. IAM automation integrates security awareness training with compliance reporting, ensuring that users acknowledge access control policies, complete security training assessments, and follow authentication security best practices. Strengthening IAM security awareness ensures that employees adhere to compliance policies, preventing audit violations and security breaches.

IAM audit preparation for SOX, GDPR, HIPAA, NIST, and ISO 27001 requires organizations to implement IAM security automation, continuous monitoring, and structured compliance reporting. By integrating IAM policy enforcement, privileged access governance, third-party identity governance, and automated audit workflows, organizations can ensure audit readiness, detect security violations, and maintain regulatory compliance. Implementing IAM security audit best practices strengthens identity governance, reduces regulatory risks, and ensures that IAM policies remain enforceable across IT environments.

IAM Compliance Documentation and Policy Development

IAM compliance documentation and policy development are essential for ensuring that organizations maintain regulatory adherence, enforce identity governance, and establish clear guidelines for access control. Compliance frameworks such as SOX, GDPR, HIPAA, NIST, and ISO 27001 require organizations to develop and maintain IAM policies that define authentication standards, access management procedures, and security enforcement mechanisms. IAM compliance documentation provides auditors, security teams, and employees with structured guidelines on identity governance, ensuring that access control policies remain enforceable across IT environments. By implementing structured IAM policy development processes, organizations can prevent security violations, mitigate identity-related risks, and ensure continuous compliance monitoring.

IAM policy development begins with defining identity governance roles, access control responsibilities, and authentication enforcement standards. Organizations must establish IAM policies that regulate user identity provisioning, privilege escalation approvals, and multi-factor authentication (MFA) enforcement. Regulatory frameworks mandate that IAM policies enforce least privilege access principles, ensuring that users receive only the necessary permissions to perform their job functions. IAM policy documentation must outline identity verification requirements, access request workflows, and privilege review procedures, ensuring that identity governance remains structured and enforceable. Automated IAM policy enforcement ensures that access control standards are consistently applied across all systems, applications, and cloud environments.

SOX compliance requires organizations to maintain IAM policies that protect financial system access, enforce privilege monitoring, and prevent unauthorized financial data modifications. IAM compliance documentation for SOX includes access certification policies, authentication logging procedures, and privileged access management

(PAM) enforcement guidelines. Organizations must document IAM access review processes, ensuring that financial system authentication logs, user access request approvals, and privilege assignment records are maintained for audit readiness. IAM automation enhances SOX compliance documentation by generating access certification reports, tracking user privilege modifications, and enforcing structured authentication policy enforcement workflows. IAM policy development for SOX ensures that financial access security controls remain aligned with regulatory mandates.

The General Data Protection Regulation (GDPR) mandates that organizations maintain IAM documentation that defines access control policies, identity governance enforcement, and data protection requirements. IAM compliance documentation for GDPR includes authentication policies, role-based access control (RBAC) enforcement procedures, and access logging guidelines for personally identifiable information (PII). Organizations must develop IAM policies that regulate data access approvals, ensuring that unauthorized users do not access PII. IAM policy documentation must outline identity verification mechanisms, data protection enforcement controls, and security incident reporting procedures. Automated IAM compliance reporting ensures that GDPR authentication logs, access review records, and identity governance enforcement policies remain structured and audit-ready.

HIPAA compliance requires healthcare organizations to document IAM security policies that regulate access to electronic protected health information (ePHI). IAM compliance documentation for HIPAA includes access provisioning policies, privileged session monitoring procedures, and identity verification requirements for medical personnel. Healthcare organizations must document IAM enforcement mechanisms that prevent unauthorized access to patient records, ensuring that authentication security policies remain aligned with HIPAA security mandates. IAM policy development for HIPAA includes defining privileged user access review processes, enforcing session monitoring requirements, and implementing authentication risk assessment procedures. Automated IAM compliance documentation ensures that ePHI access logs, privilege modification reports, and authentication validation procedures are maintained for regulatory audits.

NIST guidelines emphasize the importance of IAM policy documentation, requiring organizations to establish structured identity governance frameworks that enforce access control consistency. IAM compliance documentation for NIST includes access risk assessment policies, zero trust security enforcement guidelines, and identity authentication validation procedures. Organizations must document IAM policy enforcement workflows, ensuring that authentication anomalies, privilege escalation attempts, and access misconfigurations trigger automated security controls. IAM policy development for NIST includes defining continuous authentication policies, implementing risk-based access approval workflows, and enforcing role-based authentication validation mechanisms. Automated IAM policy reporting ensures that identity governance enforcement measures align with NIST cybersecurity mandates.

ISO 27001 mandates that organizations establish IAM policy documentation that regulates access control security, privileged access management, and identity verification enforcement. IAM compliance documentation for ISO 27001 includes access governance policies, authentication failure response procedures, and privileged session recording guidelines. Organizations must document IAM security enforcement workflows, ensuring that identity governance policies remain structured and enforceable. IAM policy development for ISO 27001 includes defining authentication monitoring procedures, enforcing privileged access validation policies, and implementing continuous compliance tracking mechanisms. Automated IAM documentation ensures that ISO 27001 authentication logs, privilege assignment records, and security incident response policies remain structured and accessible for regulatory audits.

Privileged access management (PAM) policy documentation ensures that administrative users, IT personnel, and system administrators adhere to strict IAM security controls. IAM compliance documentation for privileged access security includes privileged user authentication policies, session recording enforcement guidelines, and privileged session expiration procedures. Organizations must document IAM policy enforcement mechanisms that detect privilege misuse, ensuring that privileged accounts remain protected from unauthorized access. IAM policy development for PAM includes defining privileged access validation procedures, implementing session monitoring workflows, and enforcing just-in-time (JIT) privileged access approval processes. Automated IAM compliance documentation ensures that privileged session tracking logs, administrative authentication records, and access review reports remain structured for audit readiness.

Third-party IAM policy documentation ensures that vendors, contractors, and business partners adhere to structured authentication policies, access control requirements, and identity governance regulations. IAM compliance documentation for third-party access includes external authentication validation procedures, identity verification guidelines, and third-party session monitoring policies. Organizations must document IAM policy enforcement measures that restrict third-party access privileges, ensuring that vendor authentication credentials do not remain active beyond approved timeframes. IAM policy development for third-party compliance includes defining external access approval workflows, implementing federated authentication policies, and enforcing third-party access expiration mechanisms. Automated IAM compliance documentation ensures that third-party access monitoring logs, external user authentication reports, and vendor identity governance policies remain structured for compliance verification.

IAM compliance documentation provides organizations with structured guidelines for enforcing authentication security, access governance consistency, and privileged session monitoring. Organizations must conduct periodic IAM policy reviews, ensuring that authentication enforcement measures remain aligned with regulatory mandates. IAM automation enhances compliance documentation by generating structured policy enforcement reports, tracking IAM security violations, and enforcing real-time policy validation workflows. IAM compliance documentation ensures that organizations maintain regulatory adherence, prevent unauthorized access, and establish enforceable identity governance policies.

IAM security awareness training ensures that employees, administrators, and security teams understand IAM policy enforcement, authentication security responsibilities, and identity governance compliance requirements. Organizations must conduct IAM security training programs that educate users on access control best practices, privileged access security mandates, and regulatory compliance enforcement. IAM automation integrates compliance training with policy documentation, ensuring that users acknowledge IAM policies, complete security assessments, and follow authentication best practices. Strengthening IAM security awareness ensures that employees adhere to compliance policies, preventing security breaches and regulatory violations.

IAM compliance documentation and policy development provide organizations with structured identity governance frameworks that enforce access control security, privileged session monitoring, and authentication policy validation. By integrating IAM automation, structured policy documentation, and regulatory enforcement mechanisms, organizations can ensure compliance with SOX, GDPR, HIPAA, NIST, and ISO 27001 regulatory requirements. Implementing IAM security policy development best practices strengthens identity governance, enhances compliance verification, and ensures that IAM security policies remain enforceable across IT environments.

IAM in Financial Sector Compliance (PCI DSS, SOX)

Identity and Access Management (IAM) plays a critical role in financial sector compliance, ensuring that organizations adhere to regulatory requirements such as the Payment Card Industry Data Security Standard (PCI DSS) and the Sarbanes-Oxley Act (SOX). These regulations mandate strict access controls, authentication mechanisms, and identity governance frameworks to protect financial data, prevent fraud, and enforce accountability. IAM solutions help financial institutions manage user identities, enforce least privilege access, and monitor authentication activities to ensure regulatory compliance. By implementing IAM best practices, organizations can mitigate security risks, streamline compliance audits, and protect sensitive financial information from unauthorized access.

IAM in PCI DSS compliance requires financial institutions, payment processors, and merchants to enforce strong authentication policies that protect cardholder data. PCI DSS mandates that organizations implement multi-factor authentication (MFA) for access to payment processing systems, ensuring that unauthorized users cannot exploit weak authentication mechanisms. IAM solutions enforce PCI DSS authentication requirements by integrating with MFA providers, ensuring that users verify their identity before accessing cardholder data environments. Organizations must document IAM authentication policies, ensuring that PCI DSS access control mandates are consistently enforced. Continuous IAM monitoring detects unauthorized authentication attempts, ensuring that PCI DSS compliance remains intact.

IAM access control enforcement is critical for PCI DSS compliance, ensuring that only authorized personnel access payment processing environments. PCI DSS requires organizations to implement role-based access control (RBAC) policies that restrict payment system access to users with a legitimate business need. IAM solutions enforce RBAC policies by defining access roles, ensuring that users receive only the permissions required for their job functions. IAM compliance automation enhances PCI DSS security by detecting access anomalies, revoking unnecessary permissions, and enforcing access certification workflows that validate user entitlements. IAM reporting generates access review logs that document PCI DSS compliance, ensuring that organizations maintain audit readiness.

Privileged access management (PAM) in PCI DSS compliance ensures that administrative users do not retain excessive privileges beyond necessary job functions. PCI DSS mandates that organizations enforce privileged session monitoring, ensuring that administrative actions involving payment processing systems are logged and reviewed. IAM solutions integrate with PAM frameworks, enforcing just-in-time (JIT) privileged access provisioning, ensuring that administrators receive temporary privileges only when necessary. IAM automation enforces PCI DSS privileged access security by tracking administrative session activities, generating security alerts for unauthorized privilege escalations, and ensuring that privileged user authentication remains secure.

IAM logging and monitoring are essential for PCI DSS compliance, ensuring that all authentication attempts, access modifications, and privileged session activities are recorded. PCI DSS mandates that organizations implement centralized logging solutions that track user authentication events, detect failed login attempts, and generate real-time security alerts for unauthorized access attempts. IAM solutions enhance PCI DSS compliance by integrating with Security Information and Event Management (SIEM) systems, ensuring that authentication anomalies trigger automated remediation workflows. IAM security reporting ensures that organizations generate PCI DSS audit logs, documenting all access control policy enforcement measures for compliance verification.

IAM in SOX compliance ensures that financial institutions enforce access controls that prevent unauthorized modifications to financial reporting systems. The Sarbanes-Oxley Act mandates that organizations protect financial records from unauthorized access, requiring strict authentication, privilege management, and continuous identity monitoring. IAM compliance in SOX ensures that financial system access remains restricted to authorized personnel, preventing fraudulent activities and data manipulation. IAM policy enforcement in SOX compliance requires financial institutions to define access control policies that restrict financial system access based on job responsibilities. IAM automation enhances SOX compliance by enforcing least privilege access, preventing excessive permissions, and ensuring that financial data remains protected from unauthorized modifications.

IAM audit logging in SOX compliance ensures that organizations track financial system authentication events, access modifications, and privilege escalations. SOX mandates that organizations maintain detailed audit logs that document financial system access activities, ensuring that security teams can detect unauthorized access attempts. IAM solutions integrate with SIEM platforms, ensuring that authentication logs, access control policy violations, and privilege modification attempts are recorded and analyzed for security enforcement. IAM compliance automation in SOX generates audit-ready reports, ensuring that organizations can provide regulators with documented evidence of access policy enforcement.

IAM compliance in SOX requires organizations to implement separation of duties (SoD) policies, ensuring that financial personnel do not have conflicting access privileges that could enable fraud. IAM solutions enforce SoD policies by defining access control rules that prevent users from performing unauthorized financial transactions. IAM automation enhances SoD enforcement by detecting privilege conflicts, revoking unauthorized access permissions, and generating access review reports that document SoD compliance. IAM monitoring ensures that financial institutions prevent insider threats, ensuring that financial system authentication activities remain compliant with SOX regulations.

IAM risk assessment in financial sector compliance ensures that organizations identify authentication vulnerabilities, privilege escalation threats, and access control weaknesses before security incidents occur. PCI DSS and SOX compliance frameworks require organizations to conduct IAM risk assessments that evaluate access policy enforcement, authentication mechanism effectiveness, and privileged access security. IAM automation enhances financial sector risk management by detecting identity-related security threats, enforcing real-time authentication monitoring, and generating compliance reports that document security control effectiveness. IAM solutions integrate with security analytics platforms, ensuring that financial institutions proactively mitigate IAM security risks.

IAM training and awareness programs ensure that financial sector employees, administrators, and third-party vendors understand PCI DSS and SOX compliance requirements. Organizations must conduct IAM security training sessions that educate users on authentication best practices, access control enforcement measures, and privileged access security policies. IAM automation integrates security awareness training with authentication workflows, ensuring that users acknowledge PCI DSS and SOX policies before accessing financial systems. Strengthening IAM security awareness reduces compliance violations, preventing unauthorized financial system access and regulatory penalties.

IAM compliance in financial sector regulations such as PCI DSS and SOX requires organizations to implement structured identity governance, privileged access management, and continuous security monitoring. By enforcing IAM security policies, automating authentication enforcement, and integrating with compliance reporting solutions, financial institutions can protect payment processing environments, prevent unauthorized financial data modifications, and ensure regulatory adherence. Implementing IAM best practices in financial sector compliance strengthens identity security, reduces fraud risks, and ensures that financial organizations maintain audit-ready access governance policies.

Healthcare IAM Compliance (HIPAA, HITECH)

Identity and Access Management (IAM) plays a critical role in ensuring compliance with healthcare regulations such as the Health Insurance Portability and Accountability Act (HIPAA) and the Health Information Technology for Economic and Clinical Health Act (HITECH). These regulations mandate strict access control policies, authentication mechanisms, and identity governance frameworks to protect electronic protected health information (ePHI) from unauthorized access, misuse, and security breaches. Healthcare organizations must implement IAM solutions that enforce role-based access control (RBAC), multi-factor authentication (MFA), privileged access management (PAM), and continuous monitoring to ensure compliance with HIPAA and HITECH security requirements.

IAM policies in healthcare compliance begin with access control enforcement, ensuring that only authorized medical personnel, administrative staff, and IT professionals have access to ePHI. HIPAA mandates that healthcare providers implement technical safeguards that restrict data access based on job responsibilities. IAM solutions enforce access control policies by defining user roles, ensuring that physicians, nurses, and administrative personnel only have the necessary permissions to perform their job functions. Automated IAM policy enforcement detects excessive permissions, revokes unauthorized access, and ensures that all authentication attempts are logged for audit readiness.

MFA is a fundamental requirement for HIPAA compliance, ensuring that users authenticate their identity before accessing healthcare applications, electronic health records (EHRs), and medical databases. IAM solutions integrate with MFA providers, requiring users to verify their credentials using biometric authentication, one-time passwords (OTPs), or hardware tokens. HIPAA mandates that healthcare organizations enforce MFA for remote access, privileged accounts, and cloud-based healthcare applications. IAM automation enhances

HIPAA compliance by enforcing real-time authentication policies, detecting anomalous login attempts, and triggering security alerts for unauthorized access attempts.

Privileged access management (PAM) in healthcare IAM compliance ensures that administrative users, IT personnel, and security engineers do not retain excessive privileges beyond necessary job functions. HIPAA mandates that organizations enforce privileged session monitoring, ensuring that all administrative actions involving ePHI are tracked and reviewed. IAM solutions integrate with PAM frameworks, enforcing just-in-time (JIT) privileged access provisioning, ensuring that administrators receive temporary privileges only when necessary. IAM automation enhances HIPAA compliance by tracking privileged account activities, generating security alerts for unauthorized privilege escalations, and ensuring that privileged user authentication remains secure.

IAM compliance monitoring is essential for HITECH regulations, ensuring that healthcare organizations continuously track authentication activities, access control violations, and identity-related security incidents. HITECH expands upon HIPAA security requirements by enforcing stricter data breach notification mandates, requiring healthcare providers to report unauthorized ePHI disclosures. IAM solutions integrate with Security Information and Event Management (SIEM) systems, ensuring that authentication anomalies, access violations, and privilege modifications trigger real-time security enforcement actions. IAM automation enhances HITECH compliance by generating security alerts for unauthorized access attempts, enforcing immediate access revocation for non-compliant users, and ensuring that identity governance policies remain structured.

IAM compliance documentation is a critical component of healthcare regulatory adherence, ensuring that healthcare organizations maintain structured identity governance records, authentication logs, and privileged access review reports. HIPAA and HITECH audits require organizations to provide documented evidence of IAM policy enforcement, access review procedures, and security control effectiveness. IAM solutions generate compliance reports that track user authentication events, detect unauthorized access attempts, and document privileged session activities. Automated IAM documentation ensures that healthcare organizations maintain audit-ready compliance reports, preventing regulatory penalties and security violations.

IAM policy enforcement in HIPAA and HITECH compliance includes role-based access control (RBAC) enforcement, access certification reviews, and automated access approval workflows. Healthcare organizations must implement IAM policies that restrict ePHI access based on job responsibilities, ensuring that users do not accumulate excessive privileges over time. IAM automation enforces HIPAA access control requirements by detecting access misconfigurations, revoking unnecessary permissions, and ensuring that all authentication requests undergo policy-based access validation. IAM policy enforcement ensures that healthcare applications, patient data repositories, and medical billing systems remain protected from unauthorized access.

Third-party IAM compliance in healthcare ensures that vendors, contractors, and business partners adhere to HIPAA and HITECH authentication policies, access control mandates, and identity verification requirements. Healthcare organizations must implement IAM security measures that regulate external user access, ensuring that third-party vendors undergo strict authentication before accessing ePHI. IAM automation enforces time-limited third-party access policies, tracking vendor authentication logs, and generating security alerts for unauthorized external access attempts. IAM compliance monitoring ensures that healthcare providers maintain regulatory adherence by continuously tracking third-party access activities, enforcing secure authentication practices, and preventing unauthorized data disclosures.

IAM compliance in healthcare requires organizations to conduct periodic access reviews, ensuring that all user privileges, authentication mechanisms, and access control policies remain enforceable. HIPAA and HITECH audits assess identity governance effectiveness, requiring healthcare providers to validate user access entitlements, monitor privilege modifications, and enforce security policy adherence. IAM solutions automate access review processes, ensuring that healthcare organizations maintain real-time visibility into authentication logs, access violations, and security incidents. IAM compliance automation ensures that healthcare organizations generate structured access certification reports, documenting security policy enforcement measures and regulatory adherence.

IAM security awareness training ensures that healthcare employees, IT administrators, and security teams understand HIPAA and HITECH compliance responsibilities. Organizations must conduct IAM training programs that educate users on authentication best practices, access control enforcement measures, and privileged access security policies. IAM automation integrates security training with authentication workflows, ensuring that users acknowledge IAM policies, complete periodic compliance assessments, and follow least privilege access principles. Strengthening IAM security awareness ensures that healthcare employees adhere to compliance policies, preventing unauthorized ePHI access and data breaches.

IAM compliance enforcement in healthcare ensures that authentication security, access governance, and privileged access monitoring remain aligned with HIPAA and HITECH regulatory mandates. By integrating IAM automation, structured identity governance frameworks, and continuous security monitoring, healthcare organizations can prevent unauthorized access, mitigate insider threats, and ensure compliance with data protection requirements. Implementing IAM security best practices in healthcare strengthens ePHI security, reduces regulatory risks, and ensures that IAM policies remain enforceable across medical applications, patient databases, and healthcare IT infrastructures.

IAM in Government and Public Sector Compliance (NIST, FedRAMP)

Identity and Access Management (IAM) plays a critical role in government and public sector compliance, ensuring that agencies adhere to security standards such as the National Institute of Standards and Technology (NIST) cybersecurity framework and the Federal Risk and Authorization Management Program (FedRAMP). These regulatory frameworks mandate strict IAM controls, authentication mechanisms, and access governance policies to protect sensitive government data, prevent cyber threats, and enforce accountability. By implementing IAM solutions, government agencies can enhance security, reduce identity-related risks, and maintain compliance with NIST and FedRAMP security mandates.

IAM compliance in government begins with access control enforcement, ensuring that only authorized personnel can access government systems, classified information, and critical infrastructure. NIST mandates that government agencies implement least privilege access principles, restricting user permissions based on job responsibilities. IAM solutions enforce access control policies by defining user roles, preventing excessive privilege accumulation, and ensuring that all authentication requests undergo policy-based access validation. Automated IAM enforcement detects unauthorized access attempts, revokes excessive permissions, and ensures that access policies remain aligned with NIST security requirements.

Multi-factor authentication (MFA) is a fundamental requirement for IAM compliance in government agencies, ensuring that users verify their identity before accessing federal systems. NIST mandates that government entities enforce MFA for remote access, privileged accounts, and cloud-based applications. IAM solutions integrate with MFA providers, requiring users to authenticate using biometric verification, one-time passwords (OTPs), or smart cards. IAM automation enhances government compliance by enforcing real-time authentication policies, detecting suspicious login attempts, and triggering security alerts for unauthorized authentication failures.

Privileged access management (PAM) in government IAM compliance ensures that administrative users, IT personnel, and security engineers do not retain excessive privileges beyond necessary job functions. NIST mandates that agencies enforce privileged session monitoring, ensuring that all administrative actions involving government networks, databases, and critical infrastructure are tracked. IAM solutions integrate with PAM frameworks, enforcing just-in-time (JIT) privileged access provisioning, ensuring that administrators receive temporary privileges only when necessary. IAM automation enhances NIST compliance by tracking privileged user activities, generating security alerts for unauthorized privilege escalations, and ensuring that privileged authentication remains secure.

IAM compliance in FedRAMP ensures that government agencies and cloud service providers (CSPs) enforce strict access controls, authentication policies, and identity governance frameworks for cloud environments. FedRAMP requires CSPs to implement IAM security controls that prevent unauthorized access to government data, ensuring that authentication mechanisms comply with federal security requirements. IAM solutions enforce FedRAMP compliance by implementing continuous identity monitoring, tracking cloud authentication events, and enforcing automated access review workflows. IAM automation enhances FedRAMP security by generating security reports that document access control enforcement, authentication validation, and privileged account monitoring.

IAM monitoring is essential for government cybersecurity frameworks, ensuring that agencies continuously track authentication activities, access violations, and identity-related security incidents. NIST mandates that government agencies implement Security Information and Event Management (SIEM) solutions that detect IAM security anomalies, access control policy deviations, and authentication failures. IAM solutions integrate with SIEM platforms, ensuring that real-time authentication alerts trigger automated remediation workflows. IAM automation enhances NIST compliance by detecting unauthorized access attempts, enforcing immediate privilege revocation for non-compliant users, and ensuring that identity governance policies remain structured.

IAM compliance documentation is a critical component of government regulatory adherence, ensuring that agencies maintain structured identity governance records, authentication logs, and privileged access review reports. NIST and FedRAMP audits require organizations to provide documented evidence of IAM policy enforcement, access review procedures, and security control effectiveness. IAM solutions generate compliance reports that track user authentication events, detect unauthorized access attempts, and document privileged session activities. Automated IAM documentation ensures that government agencies maintain audit-ready compliance reports, preventing regulatory penalties and security violations.

IAM policy enforcement in government compliance includes role-based access control (RBAC) enforcement, continuous authentication monitoring, and automated access approval workflows. Government agencies must implement IAM policies that restrict system access based on security classifications, ensuring that users do not accumulate excessive privileges over time. IAM automation enforces NIST access control requirements by detecting access misconfigurations, revoking unnecessary permissions, and ensuring that all authentication requests undergo policy-based security validation. IAM policy enforcement ensures that government networks, classified information systems, and cloud environments remain protected from unauthorized access.

Third-party IAM compliance in government ensures that contractors, vendors, and external service providers adhere to NIST and FedRAMP authentication policies, access control mandates, and identity verification requirements. Agencies must implement IAM security measures that regulate external user access, ensuring that contractors undergo strict authentication before accessing government networks. IAM automation enforces time-limited third-party access policies, tracking contractor authentication logs and generating security alerts for unauthorized external access attempts. IAM compliance monitoring ensures that government entities maintain regulatory adherence by continuously tracking third-party access activities, enforcing secure authentication practices, and preventing unauthorized data disclosures.

IAM compliance in government requires agencies to conduct periodic access reviews, ensuring that all user privileges, authentication mechanisms, and access control policies remain enforceable. NIST and FedRAMP audits assess identity governance effectiveness, requiring agencies to validate user access entitlements, monitor privilege modifications, and enforce security policy adherence. IAM solutions automate access review processes, ensuring that agencies maintain real-time visibility into authentication logs, access violations, and security incidents. IAM compliance automation ensures that agencies generate structured access certification reports, documenting security policy enforcement measures and regulatory adherence.

IAM security awareness training ensures that government employees, IT administrators, and security teams understand NIST and FedRAMP compliance responsibilities. Agencies must conduct IAM training programs that educate users on authentication best practices, access control enforcement measures, and privileged access security policies. IAM automation integrates security training with authentication workflows, ensuring that users acknowledge IAM policies, complete periodic compliance assessments, and follow least privilege access principles. Strengthening IAM security awareness ensures that government employees adhere to compliance policies, preventing unauthorized access to classified information and critical systems.

IAM compliance enforcement in government ensures that authentication security, access governance, and privileged access monitoring remain aligned with NIST and FedRAMP regulatory mandates. By integrating IAM automation, structured identity governance frameworks, and continuous security monitoring, government agencies can prevent unauthorized access, mitigate insider threats, and ensure compliance with federal cybersecurity requirements. Implementing IAM security best practices in government strengthens national security, reduces cyber risks, and ensures that IAM policies remain enforceable across federal networks, cloud infrastructures, and public sector IT environments.

IAM in European Union Compliance (GDPR, eIDAS)

Identity and Access Management (IAM) plays a fundamental role in ensuring compliance with European Union regulations such as the General Data Protection Regulation (GDPR) and the Electronic Identification, Authentication, and Trust Services Regulation (eIDAS). These regulations mandate strict identity governance policies, authentication controls, and access management mechanisms to protect personal data, enforce secure digital transactions, and enhance trust in electronic identities. Organizations operating within the EU must implement IAM solutions that ensure secure access control, multi-factor authentication (MFA), and continuous monitoring of identity-related activities to maintain regulatory compliance and avoid financial penalties.

IAM compliance in GDPR is centered around the protection of personally identifiable information (PII) and the enforcement of access control policies that prevent unauthorized data exposure. Organizations must ensure that user authentication mechanisms, role-based access control (RBAC), and privilege management policies align with GDPR's data protection principles. IAM solutions enforce GDPR compliance by implementing automated access reviews, monitoring authentication attempts, and ensuring that only authorized users can access sensitive customer data. IAM automation enhances data security by detecting unauthorized access attempts, revoking excessive permissions, and generating compliance reports that document identity governance policy enforcement.

Access control enforcement in GDPR compliance ensures that personal data is accessible only to individuals who have a legitimate business need. IAM solutions enforce least privilege access policies, ensuring that employees, contractors, and third-party service providers do not retain unnecessary access rights. GDPR mandates that organizations maintain audit trails of user authentication activities, privilege modifications, and data access requests. IAM automation enforces

GDPR access control policies by generating structured compliance reports, ensuring that identity governance enforcement measures remain audit-ready. IAM monitoring detects unauthorized access attempts, enforcing real-time remediation workflows that prevent data breaches.

Multi-factor authentication (MFA) is a critical requirement for GDPR compliance, ensuring that users verify their identity before accessing sensitive personal data. IAM solutions integrate with MFA providers, enforcing biometric authentication, time-based one-time passwords (TOTP), or smart card verification. GDPR mandates that organizations implement strong authentication mechanisms for remote access, privileged accounts, and customer data processing systems. IAM automation enhances GDPR compliance by enforcing continuous authentication validation, detecting suspicious login activities, and triggering alerts for unauthorized authentication failures. Secure authentication policies ensure that organizations maintain GDPR compliance by preventing identity fraud and unauthorized data access.

IAM in eIDAS compliance ensures that organizations enforce secure electronic identification and trust services, facilitating cross-border authentication and digital identity verification within the EU. eIDAS mandates that organizations implement strong identity proofing measures, ensuring that users authenticate with legally recognized digital identities. IAM solutions enforce eIDAS compliance by integrating with national electronic identification (eID) frameworks, ensuring that authentication mechanisms align with EU trust service regulations. IAM automation enhances eIDAS security by enforcing identity verification workflows, tracking digital signature authentication logs, and ensuring that electronic transactions comply with eIDAS security mandates.

IAM privileged access management (PAM) in European Union compliance ensures that administrative users, security engineers, and IT personnel do not retain excessive privileges that could lead to unauthorized system modifications. GDPR and eIDAS mandate that organizations enforce privileged session monitoring, ensuring that administrative actions involving sensitive data and digital identity transactions are tracked. IAM solutions integrate with PAM frameworks, enforcing just-in-time (JIT) privileged access provisioning, ensuring that privileged accounts are granted temporary access only when necessary. IAM automation enhances compliance by tracking privileged account activities, generating alerts for unauthorized privilege escalations, and ensuring that privileged authentication remains secure.

IAM logging and monitoring are essential for GDPR and eIDAS compliance, ensuring that authentication activities, access modifications, and identity-related security incidents are continuously tracked. GDPR mandates that organizations implement centralized logging solutions that document all access requests, detect unauthorized authentication attempts, and generate compliance reports. IAM solutions integrate with Security Information and Event Management (SIEM) platforms, ensuring that authentication anomalies trigger automated security enforcement measures. IAM automation enhances compliance by generating security reports, enforcing access logging policies, and ensuring that organizations maintain detailed audit trails of user authentication events.

IAM compliance documentation ensures that organizations operating in the EU maintain structured identity governance records, authentication logs, and privileged access review reports. GDPR and eIDAS audits require organizations to provide documented evidence of IAM policy enforcement, authentication validation, and access control effectiveness. IAM solutions generate compliance reports that track user authentication events, detect unauthorized access attempts, and document privileged session activities. Automated IAM documentation ensures that organizations maintain audit-ready compliance reports, preventing regulatory penalties and ensuring continuous identity governance monitoring.

IAM policy enforcement in European Union compliance includes identity lifecycle management, role-based authentication policies, and automated access approval workflows. GDPR and eIDAS mandate that organizations implement IAM policies that define how digital identities are managed, ensuring that authentication workflows remain enforceable. IAM automation enforces policy compliance by detecting access misconfigurations, revoking unnecessary permissions, and ensuring that all authentication requests undergo policy-based security validation. IAM enforcement mechanisms ensure that customer identity management, electronic transactions, and access governance policies remain aligned with EU regulatory standards.

Third-party IAM compliance in the EU ensures that vendors, contractors, and business partners adhere to GDPR and eIDAS authentication policies, access control mandates, and identity verification requirements. Organizations must implement IAM security measures that regulate external user access, ensuring that third-party authentication requests comply with EU regulations. IAM automation enforces time-restricted third-party access policies, tracking vendor authentication logs and generating security alerts for unauthorized external access attempts. IAM compliance monitoring ensures that organizations maintain regulatory adherence by continuously tracking third-party access activities, enforcing secure authentication practices, and preventing unauthorized data disclosures.

IAM compliance audits provide organizations with visibility into authentication policy enforcement, access governance effectiveness, and identity verification security. GDPR and eIDAS audits assess identity governance controls, requiring organizations to validate authentication enforcement measures, monitor privileged access logs, and ensure that digital identity transactions remain secure. IAM solutions automate compliance audits by generating structured reports that track authentication activities, detect policy violations, and document regulatory adherence. IAM automation ensures that organizations maintain EU compliance by enforcing access control policies, monitoring authentication security, and preventing identity-related security risks.

IAM security awareness training ensures that employees,

administrators, and security teams understand GDPR and eIDAS compliance responsibilities. Organizations must conduct IAM training programs that educate users on authentication best practices, data access regulations, and privileged access security policies. IAM automation integrates security training with authentication workflows, ensuring that users acknowledge IAM policies, complete periodic compliance assessments, and follow secure authentication principles. Strengthening IAM security awareness ensures that employees adhere to compliance policies, preventing unauthorized data access and identity-related security breaches.

IAM compliance enforcement in the European Union ensures that authentication security, access governance, and privileged access monitoring remain aligned with GDPR and eIDAS regulatory mandates. By integrating IAM automation, structured identity governance frameworks, and continuous security monitoring, organizations can prevent unauthorized access, mitigate identity fraud risks, and ensure compliance with EU data protection requirements. Implementing IAM security best practices in European compliance strengthens digital identity security, reduces regulatory risks, and ensures that IAM policies remain enforceable across multinational organizations, cloud environments, and digital service providers.

Future Trends in IAM Audit and Compliance

The evolving landscape of cybersecurity, regulatory requirements, and digital transformation is shaping the future of Identity and Access Management (IAM) audit and compliance. As organizations adopt new technologies, expand their cloud presence, and integrate artificial intelligence (AI) into security operations, IAM frameworks must adapt to ensure continuous regulatory adherence and protection against emerging threats. Future IAM trends focus on automation, AI-driven analytics, Zero Trust security models, decentralized identity management, and enhanced compliance reporting mechanisms. These advancements will strengthen IAM audit processes, improve identity governance, and enhance security enforcement across complex IT environments.

The increasing reliance on automation in IAM compliance will redefine how organizations conduct identity audits, enforce access policies, and manage privileged accounts. Automated IAM audit tools will replace traditional manual review processes, enabling real-time access certification, role validation, and policy enforcement. Organizations will integrate IAM solutions with robotic process automation (RPA) and security orchestration, automation, and response (SOAR) platforms to detect access anomalies, enforce compliance policies, and generate audit reports with minimal human intervention. Automated IAM compliance will reduce operational overhead, minimize audit discrepancies, and ensure continuous adherence to regulatory frameworks such as SOX, GDPR, HIPAA, NIST, and ISO 27001.

AI and machine learning will play a crucial role in IAM audit and compliance, transforming identity governance by enabling predictive access control, behavior-based authentication, and anomaly detection. AI-driven IAM analytics will assess user behavior, detect privilege misuse, and enforce dynamic risk-based access policies. Organizations will leverage AI to analyze authentication patterns, identify suspicious activities, and automatically revoke access when security threats are detected. AI-powered IAM solutions will enhance compliance reporting by correlating access events, detecting policy violations, and generating real-time audit insights. The integration of AI into IAM will improve security decision-making, reduce false positives, and streamline compliance validation processes.

The adoption of Zero Trust security models will reshape IAM compliance by enforcing continuous authentication, micro-segmentation, and identity-based access policies. Organizations will implement Zero Trust principles to ensure that users and devices must always authenticate and validate their identity before accessing corporate resources. IAM solutions will integrate with Zero Trust frameworks to enforce just-in-time (JIT) access provisioning, adaptive authentication, and identity risk scoring. Future IAM audit processes will assess Zero Trust policy enforcement, tracking authentication events, privilege modifications, and access violations in real time. Zero Trust IAM compliance will prevent unauthorized access, enhance identity governance, and strengthen regulatory adherence.

The emergence of decentralized identity management will introduce new IAM compliance challenges and opportunities. Decentralized identity frameworks, powered by blockchain technology, will enable users to control their digital identities without relying on centralized authentication providers. Organizations will need to update IAM audit processes to validate decentralized identity credentials, ensuring that authentication transactions comply with regulatory requirements. Future IAM compliance audits will assess how decentralized identities are issued, stored, and verified within digital ecosystems. The adoption of self-sovereign identity (SSI) models will require organizations to redefine identity governance policies, enforce cryptographic authentication mechanisms, and integrate decentralized identity verification into IAM frameworks.

Cloud IAM compliance will continue to evolve as organizations expand their cloud-based infrastructure and integrate multi-cloud identity governance solutions. Future IAM audit trends will focus on ensuring that cloud access policies, authentication mechanisms, and identity federation models remain aligned with regulatory requirements. Organizations will adopt cloud-native IAM solutions that provide centralized visibility into cloud authentication events, privilege assignments, and access violations. IAM automation will enable organizations to enforce cloud compliance by detecting misconfigured identity settings, generating cloud access certification reports, and applying automated remediation workflows. Cloud IAM compliance will require enhanced security monitoring, continuous audit validation, and policy-based enforcement mechanisms to mitigate cloud-related identity risks.

Regulatory compliance standards will continue to evolve, introducing new IAM audit requirements, security mandates, and identity governance policies. Future IAM compliance frameworks will incorporate stricter access control guidelines, requiring organizations to enforce enhanced authentication protocols, biometric identity verification, and behavioral access controls. Compliance audits will demand more transparency in identity lifecycle management, requiring organizations to track user access from initial provisioning to deactivation. IAM solutions will integrate with compliance management platforms to automate regulatory reporting, ensuring that organizations can provide auditors with real-time evidence of IAM policy enforcement.

IAM risk-based authentication will become a standard compliance requirement, ensuring that user authentication events are continuously evaluated based on contextual risk factors. Future IAM solutions will assess authentication risks by analyzing device trust levels, login locations, behavioral biometrics, and historical access trends. IAM compliance audits will require organizations to document risk-based access decisions, ensuring that authentication policies adapt dynamically to changing threat environments. AI-powered risk analysis will enhance IAM security by preventing unauthorized access, mitigating insider threats, and ensuring that authentication policies remain compliant with evolving regulatory standards.

The convergence of IAM and identity threat detection will introduce new compliance validation techniques, requiring organizations to implement identity-centric security analytics, forensic investigations, and incident response automation. Future IAM compliance audits will assess how organizations detect and respond to identity-based threats, ensuring that authentication anomalies trigger real-time security controls. IAM solutions will integrate with threat intelligence platforms to detect credential-based attacks, phishing attempts, and unauthorized privilege escalations. Identity threat detection compliance will require organizations to maintain audit logs of identity-related security incidents, ensuring that IAM security measures remain enforceable.

Enhanced IAM compliance dashboards and reporting mechanisms will improve audit transparency, enabling organizations to track access governance metrics, authentication trends, and compliance violations in real time. Future IAM solutions will provide interactive compliance dashboards that display identity risk assessments, user privilege audits, and security policy enforcement metrics. Automated IAM reporting will enable organizations to generate audit-ready compliance documentation, ensuring that regulators, auditors, and security teams have access to real-time IAM insights. Organizations will leverage compliance analytics to assess IAM policy effectiveness, identify security gaps, and optimize identity governance strategies.

The integration of IAM with emerging security technologies such as passwordless authentication, identity federation, and continuous authentication will introduce new compliance requirements and audit validation techniques. Organizations will implement passwordless IAM solutions that leverage biometrics, cryptographic keys, and identity-bound authentication tokens to eliminate reliance on traditional credentials. Future IAM compliance audits will assess the effectiveness of passwordless authentication policies, ensuring that organizations enforce strong identity verification mechanisms. Identity federation compliance will require organizations to validate federated authentication transactions, ensuring that third-party identity providers adhere to regulatory security standards. Continuous authentication compliance will demand real-time monitoring of user behavior, ensuring that authentication policies remain adaptive and risk-aware.

Future trends in IAM audit and compliance will focus on automation, AI-driven security analytics, Zero Trust enforcement, decentralized identity management, and cloud-native IAM governance. Organizations must adopt advanced IAM compliance frameworks, integrate identity risk assessments, and enforce continuous security monitoring to align with evolving regulatory mandates. By leveraging IAM automation, AI-powered analytics, and risk-based authentication, organizations can enhance identity governance, prevent unauthorized access, and ensure regulatory adherence across dynamic IT ecosystems. IAM audit processes will become more adaptive, data-driven, and security-centric, ensuring that identity compliance frameworks remain resilient in the face of emerging cybersecurity threats and regulatory challenges.

The Role of AI and Machine Learning in IAM Compliance

Artificial Intelligence (AI) and Machine Learning (ML) are transforming Identity and Access Management (IAM) compliance by enabling organizations to enhance security, automate identity governance, and improve threat detection. Traditional IAM compliance models rely on static rules and manual audits, which often fail to adapt to evolving cyber threats and regulatory requirements. AI-driven IAM solutions introduce dynamic access control, real-time risk assessment, and intelligent automation to streamline compliance with regulations such as SOX, GDPR, HIPAA, NIST, and ISO 27001. By integrating AI and ML into IAM frameworks, organizations can ensure continuous compliance enforcement, prevent unauthorized access, and mitigate identity-related security risks.

AI-powered IAM solutions enhance authentication security by analyzing user behavior, detecting anomalies, and enforcing adaptive authentication policies. Traditional multi-factor authentication (MFA) relies on fixed verification steps, but AI-driven authentication systems assess contextual factors such as login patterns, device reputation, and geographic locations to determine authentication risk levels. Machine learning algorithms continuously learn from authentication attempts, identifying suspicious login behaviors and triggering additional security measures when anomalies are detected. AI-driven authentication enhances compliance by ensuring that access control policies adapt dynamically to evolving security threats, reducing the risk of credential-based attacks and unauthorized access attempts.

Role-based access control (RBAC) and attribute-based access control (ABAC) benefit from AI and ML capabilities that optimize identity governance and enforce least privilege access policies. Traditional IAM models rely on predefined roles and static access rules, leading to privilege creep and excessive permissions. AI-driven IAM solutions analyze access patterns, detect over-provisioned accounts, and recommend privilege adjustments based on real-time risk assessments.

Machine learning models assess historical access trends, ensuring that users receive only the permissions necessary for their job functions. Automated role optimization enhances compliance by preventing excessive privilege accumulation and enforcing dynamic access governance policies that align with regulatory requirements.

Privileged access management (PAM) benefits from AI-driven threat detection and real-time anomaly monitoring. Privileged accounts are high-value targets for cybercriminals, making PAM compliance a critical component of IAM security. AI-powered PAM solutions monitor privileged session activities, detect unauthorized privilege escalations, and enforce automated access revocation when suspicious behaviors are identified. Machine learning models analyze privileged account activities, distinguishing between legitimate administrative actions and potential security threats. AI-driven risk scoring enhances compliance by ensuring that privileged access policies remain enforceable, reducing the risk of insider threats and unauthorized system modifications.

IAM compliance audits are significantly improved through AI-powered automation and intelligent compliance reporting. Traditional IAM audits require organizations to manually review access logs, track authentication attempts, and validate policy enforcement measures. AI-driven IAM solutions automate compliance audits by analyzing authentication data, detecting policy violations, and generating audit-ready compliance reports. Machine learning algorithms identify access anomalies, ensuring that security teams receive real-time alerts for IAM policy deviations. AI-driven compliance automation reduces the administrative burden of IAM audits, ensuring that organizations maintain regulatory adherence without manual intervention.

AI and ML enhance real-time access monitoring by detecting behavioral anomalies and identifying unauthorized access attempts. Traditional IAM monitoring systems rely on predefined rules, which often fail to detect sophisticated identity threats. AI-powered identity analytics assess user behavior patterns, detecting deviations from normal authentication trends and triggering automated security responses. Machine learning models continuously analyze authentication data, identifying insider threats, compromised credentials, and privilege abuse in real time. AI-driven anomaly detection enhances compliance by ensuring that security teams receive proactive alerts for identity-related security incidents, preventing unauthorized access before compliance violations occur.

Third-party IAM compliance benefits from AI-driven identity verification and risk assessment models. Organizations frequently grant external vendors, contractors, and business partners access to internal systems, increasing the risk of security breaches. AI-powered IAM solutions assess third-party authentication risks, ensuring that external users comply with access control policies. Machine learning models analyze vendor authentication patterns, detecting suspicious access attempts and enforcing adaptive security measures. AI-driven third-party IAM compliance enhances regulatory adherence by ensuring that vendor identities are continuously verified, access privileges are dynamically adjusted, and unauthorized third-party activities are detected in real time.

AI-driven IAM automation simplifies identity lifecycle management by dynamically provisioning and deprovisioning user accounts based on contextual risk factors. Traditional IAM workflows require manual user provisioning and access certification reviews, leading to delays in access approvals and security misconfigurations. AI-powered IAM solutions automate identity lifecycle processes by analyzing user roles, predicting access requirements, and enforcing real-time provisioning policies. Machine learning models assess employment status changes, detecting role transitions and automatically adjusting user permissions. AI-driven identity lifecycle automation enhances compliance by ensuring that IAM policies remain enforceable, preventing orphan accounts and unauthorized access retention.

Regulatory frameworks such as GDPR, HIPAA, and NIST mandate that organizations implement risk-based authentication and continuous compliance monitoring. AI and ML enhance risk-based authentication by dynamically assessing login attempts, assigning risk scores to authentication events, and enforcing adaptive access control measures. AI-powered IAM compliance solutions continuously analyze authentication logs, detecting deviations from normal behavior and triggering real-time security enforcement mechanisms. Machine learning-driven risk assessments enhance compliance by ensuring that IAM policies remain adaptive, preventing unauthorized access attempts and reducing regulatory risks.

IAM threat intelligence is improved through AI-driven security analytics that detect credential-based attacks, phishing attempts, and identity fraud. Traditional IAM security models struggle to detect emerging threats due to reliance on static security rules. AI-powered IAM solutions integrate with threat intelligence platforms, analyzing authentication data to identify compromised credentials and suspicious login behaviors. Machine learning models predict identity fraud patterns, enabling organizations to implement proactive security measures before compliance violations occur. AI-driven IAM threat intelligence enhances regulatory adherence by ensuring that organizations detect and mitigate identity-related security threats in real time.

IAM compliance dashboards and reporting mechanisms are revolutionized through AI-powered analytics that provide real-time insights into identity governance metrics, access violations, and authentication trends. Traditional IAM reporting systems generate static compliance reports, limiting visibility into security incidents. AI-driven IAM dashboards offer dynamic compliance analytics, enabling organizations to assess identity risk levels, monitor access control effectiveness, and detect policy deviations in real time. Machine learning models provide predictive analytics, identifying emerging compliance risks before regulatory audits occur. AI-driven compliance reporting enhances IAM security by ensuring that organizations maintain continuous visibility into identity governance enforcement.

The integration of AI and ML into IAM compliance frameworks is redefining how organizations enforce access control policies, detect identity threats, and automate compliance auditing. AI-driven IAM solutions enhance authentication security, optimize role-based access governance, and streamline identity lifecycle management. Machine learning models improve privileged access monitoring, detect third-party authentication risks, and automate compliance reporting. AI-powered IAM compliance ensures that organizations remain resilient against identity-related security threats, maintain regulatory adherence, and proactively mitigate access control risks in an evolving digital landscape.

Case Studies of IAM Compliance Successes and Failures

IAM compliance plays a crucial role in securing organizations against unauthorized access, data breaches, and regulatory violations. Organizations that successfully implement IAM frameworks aligned with regulations such as SOX, GDPR, HIPAA, NIST, and ISO 27001 demonstrate resilience against security threats and achieve streamlined compliance auditing. However, failures in IAM implementation have led to severe security incidents, financial penalties, and reputational damage. Examining case studies of IAM compliance successes and failures provides valuable insights into best practices, common pitfalls, and lessons learned.

A major financial institution successfully enhanced IAM compliance by implementing automated identity governance and privileged access management (PAM). Facing regulatory scrutiny under SOX, the bank conducted an IAM risk assessment that revealed excessive privileged accounts, orphaned credentials, and inadequate access review processes. The organization adopted an AI-driven IAM solution that enforced least privilege access, automated access reviews, and implemented real-time authentication monitoring. Multi-factor authentication (MFA) was mandated for all privileged users, and just-in-time (JIT) privileged access provisioning reduced the risk of standing administrative privileges. Within a year, audit readiness improved significantly, and compliance reporting became fully automated. The successful IAM deployment led to a reduction in access violations, improved regulatory adherence, and enhanced protection of financial data.

A healthcare provider suffered a data breach due to inadequate IAM compliance under HIPAA regulations. The organization failed to enforce proper authentication controls for remote healthcare professionals accessing electronic protected health information (ePHI). The breach resulted from compromised credentials that lacked MFA, allowing unauthorized access to sensitive patient data. Post-incident investigations revealed that privileged access was not adequately monitored, and session logging was insufficient. Regulatory fines were imposed due to non-compliance, prompting the organization to overhaul its IAM framework. The healthcare provider implemented a comprehensive IAM solution that enforced role-based access control (RBAC), real-time privilege monitoring, and biometric authentication for remote access. The organization achieved full HIPAA compliance, prevented further breaches, and improved IAM governance across all healthcare facilities.

A multinational technology company successfully navigated GDPR compliance challenges by implementing a robust IAM strategy that prioritized data protection and access control enforcement. The company faced issues with excessive user permissions, uncontrolled third-party access, and a lack of identity lifecycle management. By integrating IAM automation, the company enforced stringent authentication requirements, implemented user activity monitoring, and adopted federated identity management for secure third-party authentication. The IAM framework ensured that all personally identifiable information (PII) access requests were logged, reviewed, and approved based on strict GDPR guidelines. The organization passed GDPR audits with no violations, reducing compliance risks and strengthening data security across its European operations.

A government agency experienced an IAM compliance failure due to misconfigured identity and access controls, leading to unauthorized access to classified data. The agency relied on outdated IAM policies that did not align with NIST security standards, resulting in unmonitored privileged accounts and weak authentication policies. An internal audit revealed that employees retained access to sensitive systems long after their roles had changed, increasing insider threat risks. Following the compliance failure, the agency implemented an IAM transformation strategy, introducing automated deprovisioning, continuous identity risk assessment, and zero trust security enforcement. The upgraded IAM framework ensured that access controls met NIST compliance requirements, reducing insider threats and enhancing security posture across government networks.

A global retail company successfully navigated PCI DSS compliance by strengthening its IAM security framework. The organization faced challenges with securing payment processing systems, enforcing privileged access controls, and managing third-party authentication risks. A compliance audit identified gaps in access governance, including shared administrative accounts and inadequate authentication mechanisms for financial transactions. The company implemented a centralized IAM solution that enforced MFA for all payment system users, implemented PAM to secure administrative privileges, and introduced continuous access monitoring. Real-time identity analytics detected and mitigated unauthorized access attempts, ensuring that all PCI DSS security requirements were met. As a result, the organization improved fraud prevention, enhanced customer data protection, and maintained a strong compliance posture across its global retail operations.

A cloud service provider failed to comply with FedRAMP security requirements due to poor IAM implementation, leading to delays in obtaining federal authorization. The organization struggled with enforcing access control consistency across multiple cloud environments, resulting in identity governance failures. An assessment revealed excessive permissions for cloud administrators, lack of privileged session monitoring, and an absence of automated access certification workflows. The company restructured its IAM framework by integrating cloud-native identity management, enforcing role-based authentication policies, and implementing AI-driven access anomaly detection. The IAM transformation resulted in FedRAMP compliance approval, allowing the company to provide cloud services to government agencies while maintaining strict security controls.

A European financial services company faced severe penalties for IAM non-compliance under GDPR due to improper handling of user identity data. The company stored authentication logs without adequate encryption, failed to enforce access logging policies, and did not implement identity verification controls for customer account recovery processes. A data protection audit identified compliance violations, resulting in regulatory fines and reputational damage. To address the issues, the organization adopted an IAM solution that ensured encrypted authentication storage, enforced MFA for account recovery, and implemented identity analytics to detect fraudulent activities. The IAM compliance overhaul restored regulatory adherence, strengthened customer data protection, and improved trust in financial transactions.

An energy sector company successfully implemented IAM security controls aligned with ISO 27001, improving resilience against cyber threats and compliance violations. The organization faced challenges in enforcing authentication security, managing privileged access, and securing third-party identities within critical infrastructure networks. By deploying an IAM automation framework, the company ensured continuous monitoring of user authentication events, implemented JIT privileged access controls, and enforced adaptive authentication for remote users. IAM analytics provided real-time security insights, enabling proactive identity threat detection and policy enforcement. The organization achieved ISO 27001 certification, reduced operational security risks, and improved compliance readiness across energy infrastructure systems.

A major airline suffered an IAM compliance failure due to weak identity verification processes, resulting in fraudulent access to customer accounts and financial data breaches. The company relied on static passwords without enforcing MFA, allowing attackers to exploit compromised credentials. An investigation revealed gaps in identity lifecycle management, where former employees retained access to internal airline systems. Following the breach, the airline adopted a zero trust IAM model that enforced biometric authentication, implemented continuous risk-based access assessments, and automated account deprovisioning. IAM improvements restored compliance with regulatory standards, improved customer data security, and enhanced fraud prevention capabilities.

IAM compliance successes and failures demonstrate the importance of proactive identity governance, strong authentication mechanisms, and continuous access monitoring. Organizations that successfully implement IAM automation, privileged access security, and real-time compliance reporting can mitigate security risks, enhance regulatory adherence, and maintain strong identity protection. Examining real-world case studies provides valuable insights into IAM best practices, reinforcing the need for continuous improvements in identity security frameworks.

Final Thoughts on IAM Audit, Compliance, and Continuous Improvement

Identity and Access Management (IAM) audit and compliance play a central role in modern cybersecurity strategies, ensuring that organizations maintain control over access to critical systems and data while adhering to regulatory requirements. As businesses continue to expand their digital footprints, the need for strong IAM frameworks becomes even more critical. Compliance mandates such as SOX, GDPR, HIPAA, NIST, and ISO 27001 require organizations to enforce strict identity governance, access control policies, and authentication mechanisms. Beyond achieving initial compliance, organizations must focus on continuous improvement in IAM to keep pace with evolving threats, regulatory updates, and technological advancements.

The foundation of effective IAM compliance lies in robust authentication, authorization, and access management policies. Organizations must implement multi-factor authentication (MFA), role-based access control (RBAC), and privilege management to mitigate identity-related security risks. Enforcing the principle of least privilege ensures that users only have access to the resources necessary for their job functions, reducing the risk of insider threats and unauthorized access. IAM solutions provide automated workflows for access approvals, privilege escalations, and deprovisioning, helping organizations maintain compliance with minimal administrative overhead. Continuous monitoring of authentication events, privilege modifications, and session activities further strengthens compliance readiness and risk mitigation efforts.

IAM audits serve as a critical mechanism for evaluating access control effectiveness, detecting policy violations, and ensuring compliance adherence. Regular IAM audits provide organizations with insights into authentication patterns, access anomalies, and privilege misuse, allowing security teams to take corrective actions before security incidents occur. Automated IAM auditing solutions integrate with Security Information and Event Management (SIEM) platforms to generate real-time compliance reports, ensuring that organizations remain audit-ready at all times. Conducting periodic IAM risk assessments enables organizations to identify security gaps, evaluate policy enforcement effectiveness, and align identity governance strategies with regulatory requirements.

Continuous improvement in IAM compliance requires organizations to embrace automation, artificial intelligence (AI), and machine learning (ML) to enhance identity governance efficiency. AI-driven IAM solutions analyze user behavior, detect authentication anomalies, and recommend adaptive access control measures based on risk assessments. By integrating AI into IAM frameworks, organizations can reduce false positives in authentication monitoring, optimize role-based access assignments, and enforce intelligent security policies. AI-powered compliance analytics enable organizations to predict emerging IAM risks, ensuring that identity governance remains proactive rather than reactive. Leveraging AI and ML for IAM compliance enhances security decision-making, minimizes human error, and streamlines identity governance operations.

Privileged access management (PAM) is a crucial component of IAM compliance, as privileged accounts present significant security risks if not properly managed. Organizations must enforce strict privileged access policies, including just-in-time (JIT) access provisioning, privileged session monitoring, and automatic privilege revocation for inactive accounts. PAM automation ensures that privileged users do not retain excessive permissions, reducing the likelihood of privilege abuse and insider threats. IAM compliance frameworks mandate continuous monitoring of privileged account activities, ensuring that administrative actions are logged, reviewed, and audited for security violations. Strengthening privileged access security is essential for maintaining compliance with SOX, HIPAA, and other regulatory mandates.

Third-party IAM compliance remains a critical challenge for organizations that grant external vendors, contractors, and business partners access to internal systems. Organizations must implement federated identity management, third-party authentication monitoring, and access expiration policies to mitigate risks associated with external identity governance. Automated IAM solutions enforce time-limited third-party access permissions, track vendor authentication logs, and generate compliance alerts for unauthorized external access attempts. By integrating third-party identity risk management into IAM frameworks, organizations can maintain compliance while ensuring that external users adhere to strict authentication policies and access governance controls.

Cloud IAM compliance continues to evolve as organizations transition to multi-cloud and hybrid IT environments. Ensuring that cloud identities remain secure and compliant requires organizations to adopt cloud-native IAM solutions that provide centralized visibility into cloud authentication events, access policies, and identity federation models. IAM automation enables organizations to enforce cloud compliance by detecting misconfigured identity settings, generating real-time access certification reports, and applying automated remediation workflows for cloud security violations. Cloud IAM governance ensures that identity-based security policies remain consistent across on-premises and cloud infrastructures, preventing unauthorized access to sensitive cloud-hosted applications and data.

Zero Trust security models have become an essential strategy for improving IAM compliance and access control enforcement. Zero Trust principles require organizations to continuously validate user identities, enforce adaptive authentication policies, and implement micro-segmentation to limit lateral movement within networks. IAM solutions integrate with Zero Trust architectures to enforce risk-based authentication, behavior-based access controls, and identity verification workflows. Implementing Zero Trust IAM compliance enhances security resilience by ensuring that users and devices are continuously authenticated, reducing the risk of credential-based attacks and unauthorized privilege escalations.

Regulatory frameworks and compliance standards will continue to evolve, requiring organizations to adapt their IAM strategies to meet new security mandates. Future IAM compliance requirements may introduce stricter authentication policies, enhanced data protection controls, and expanded identity verification measures. Organizations must stay informed about regulatory updates, ensuring that IAM policies remain aligned with emerging compliance trends. Continuous IAM policy reviews, security training programs, and IAM automation enhancements will be necessary to maintain compliance readiness and protect against identity-related security threats.

IAM compliance is not a one-time achievement but an ongoing process that requires continuous monitoring, policy enforcement, and technological innovation. Organizations must prioritize IAM strategy refinement, invest in security automation, and conduct regular access certification reviews to stay ahead of evolving compliance challenges. The integration of IAM with AI-driven analytics, Zero Trust security, and automated identity governance ensures that organizations can maintain compliance while improving security resilience.

IAM audit and compliance will remain a cornerstone of cybersecurity as organizations navigate an increasingly complex threat landscape. The ability to enforce dynamic access controls, implement real-time authentication monitoring, and detect identity-based security risks will determine an organization's compliance success. By adopting IAM best practices, leveraging automation, and embracing continuous improvement, organizations can achieve long-term IAM compliance, strengthen identity security, and protect critical assets from unauthorized access.

www.ingramcontent.com/pod-product-compliance
Lightning Source LLC
LaVergne TN
LVHW022308060326
832902LV00020B/3331